ETERNAL REST IN THE LORD

Preparing the Liturgy of the Word at Catholic Funerals

Paul H. Colloton, OSFS

Mary G. Fox

Corinna Laughlin

Lorie Simmons

LITURGY
TRAINING
PUBLICATIONS

Nihil Obstat
Reverend Mr. Daniel G. Welter, JD
Chancellor
Archdiocese of Chicago
April 4, 2018

Imprimatur
Most Reverend Francis J. Kane, DD
Vicar General
Archdiocese of Chicago
April 4, 2018

The *Nihil Obstat* and *Imprimatur* are official declarations that a book is free of doctrinal and moral error. No implication is contained therein that those who have granted the *Nihil Obstat* and *Imprimatur* agree with the content, opinions, or statements expressed. Nor do they assume any legal responsibility associated with publication.

This book was edited by Danielle A. Noe, MDiv. Michael A. Dodd was the production editor, and Kari Nicholls was the designer and the production artist.

Cover image © The Crosiers/Gene Plaisted, OSC, of Reinarts stained glass window at Holy Family Church, St. Louis Park, Minnesota.

Printed in the United States of America.

22 21 20 19 18   1 2 3 4 5

Library of Congress Control Number: 2018936995

ISBN 978-1-61671-424-6

EERL

Preparing the Liturgy of the Word at Catholic Funerals

Merciful Lord,

turn toward us and listen to our prayers:

open the gates of paradise to your servant

and help us who remain

to comfort one another with assurance of faith,

until we all meet in Christ . . .

—*Order of Christian Funerals*, 202

We offer you our sympathy as you prepare to celebrate the funeral rites of the Catholic Church in memory of your loved one. *Eternal Rest in the Lord* has been written to assist you in preparing the Liturgy of the Word at a Catholic funeral liturgy (within or without Mass). There are choices for you to make. These choices help those who gather reflect on your loved one's life in light of her or his union with Christ's life, death, and Resurrection. The Church encourages you to make these choices with the priest, deacon, or pastoral minister with whom you will prepare the funeral liturgy. This book will help you select the readings for the liturgy and write the Prayer of the Faithful.

The Liturgy of the Word during the Catholic Funeral Liturgy

Every Catholic funeral—whether celebrated within Mass or without Mass, for deceased adults, baptized or unbaptized children—includes the Liturgy of the Word, in which readings from Scripture and prayers for general needs are offered (the Prayer of the Faithful). The readings remind us about the Paschal Mystery, that is, Christ's death and Resurrection. They remind us to remember those who have died in the light of hope, since God created us for union with God. We gather to express our faith that one day we hope to be reunited with our deceased loved ones in the kingdom of heaven. The readings and the Prayer of the Faithful offer strength and comfort and encourage us to witness our belief that for God's faithful ones, life is changed, not ended.

The Liturgy of the Word at a Catholic funeral essentially follows the same order as Sunday Mass (there is no Creed at a Catholic funeral).

✢ **The First Reading***   1

✢ **The Responsorial Psalm**   17

✢ **The Second Reading**   29

✢ **The Alleluia Verse and Verse before
    the Gospel (Gospel Acclamation)**   49

✢ **The Gospel**   51

✢ **Homily**

✢ **The Prayer of the Faithful**   115

Funerals for Children Who Have Died

There is certainly nothing more tragic than the loss of a child. Be assured of the Church's prayers, support, and consolation. The Church provides special readings for funeral liturgies celebrated for children who were baptized or who died before they were baptized. These readings are also found in this resource:

✢ **Baptized Children**   81

✢ **Children Who Died before Baptism**   105

---

* The First Reading is usually from the Old Testament except during Easter Time. During Easter Time, readings from the Acts of the Apostles or the Book of Revelation are chosen (**see pages 11–16, FRE–1 to FRE–4**).

Using Eternal Rest in the Lord

Eternal Rest in the Lord is designed to assist you in choosing the readings and writing the Prayer of the Faithful for the funeral liturgy of your loved one. This might be the first time you are choosing readings or writing prayers for a liturgy, whether it is celebrated within Mass or without Mass (these same readings may also be chosen for services taking place at the Vigil, wake, or visitation). If it is your first time doing this, you are not alone. This resource, and the priest, deacon, or pastoral minister with whom you are meeting, are all here to help you.

We invite you to make this as prayerful an experience as possible. Think about the person whose life you will honor during the funeral liturgy. Read each option from which you are to choose a First or Second Reading, Responsorial Psalm, Gospel Acclamation, or Gospel. Think about how that reading reflects or honors the life of the person as you knew her or him. Think about how the reading honors the person's life of faith. Think about the people who will gather for the funeral liturgy. Think about how those who are grieving need comfort from the Scripture texts that are proclaimed. Ask the Holy Spirit to help you choose a reading that brings together all of the points that you thought about when reflecting upon the readings. Then choose that reading to be proclaimed at the liturgy when you gather to remember and pray for your loved one.

This book includes:

+ background information and reflections on each reading to help you select texts that echo your love for the deceased person and your faith in God;

+ an at-a-glance reference that offers reasons about why you might select that reading, to help you connect it to the life of your loved one, and what might help you find comfort at this time of need;

+ suggestions for other readings that fit well together;

+ sample Prayer of the Faithful with tips to help you write your own prayers;

✦ a form for you to complete that tells the presider which readings you have chosen. It is found on page 121. You may also download this file from www.LTP.org/s/EERL_form. To access the editable PDF click on the "Supplement" tab.

When we gather for the funeral of a member of the Body of Christ we offer God worship and praise. We thank God for the gift of your loved one, whose life is being returned to God, our creator and our hope. We commend your loved one to God's merciful love and ask forgiveness for any sins she or he may have committed in this life. We express the fact that the Church on earth is united with the Church in heaven, so we continue to be united with your loved one, but in a new way. Because of that new way, we need to honor the pain that comes from no longer being able to see, hear, touch, and feel the physical presence of your loved one. We gather to offer consolation to you and all who will miss the person whose life we honor and to find hope in the rituals that the Church gives us at this time on our life journey. We invite you to choose readings and prayers that will help you to be consoled, find hope in the promise of the Resurrection, and experience the support of the community who will gather with you.

The First Reading from the Old Testament

At Catholic funerals celebrated outside of Easter Time, the First Reading comes from the Old Testament. There are seven Old Testament readings from which to choose, found in this chapter numbered **FR–1**, **FR–2**, and so on. The readings at a funeral liturgy may not be replaced with non-biblical readings.

Some readings may sound familiar to you. Others may be new to you. Take some time to read the passages in light of your loved one's life and consider your families' needs at this time. Choose the reading that helps you hear God speak to you, offering comfort, hope, and faith in the Resurrection.

During Easter Time, readings from the New Testament are chosen as the First Reading. Refer to **pages 11–16**.

If you are not sure what reading to choose, your pastor or whomever you are meeting with to prepare the funeral can help.

FR-1

He acted in an excellent and noble way as he had the resurrection of the dead in view.

A reading from the second Book of Maccabees   *12:43–46*

Judas, the ruler of Israel,
   took up a collection among all his soldiers,
   amounting to two thousand silver drachmas,
   which he sent to Jerusalem to provide for an expiatory sacrifice.
In doing this he acted in a very excellent and noble way,
   inasmuch as he had the resurrection of the dead in view;
   for if he were not expecting the fallen to rise again,
   it would have been useless and foolish to pray for them in death.
But if he did this with a view to the splendid reward
   that awaits those who had gone to rest in godliness,
   it was a holy and pious thought.
Thus he made atonement for the dead
   that they might be freed from this sin.

The word of the Lord.

Background of the Reading

This reading addresses the author's belief in the afterlife and the resurrection of the body, as expressed by Judas' collection to pray for the dead. Those who die with faith will rise again. If this were not true: "it would have been useless and foolish to pray for them in death" (44). This is our belief, too. Our belief in the resurrection offers hope that our deceased loved ones will share eternal life by being freed from sin.

You might select this reading because your loved one . . .

sacrificed for others • was a noble individual who looked out for those who could not look out for themselves • was a civic leader who worked for the good of others.

If you select this reading, you might also consider . . .

Psalm 42:2, 3, 5cdef, 43:3, 4, 5 **(RP-4)** • Romans 6:3–9 or 6:3–4, 8–9 **(SR-3)** • Matthew 25:1–13 **(G-3)**

FR–2

I know that my vindicator lives.

A reading from the Book of Job   *19:1, 23–27a*

Job answered Bildad the Shuhite and said:
Oh, would that my words were written down!
  Would that they were inscribed in a record:
That with an iron chisel and with lead
  they were cut in the rock forever!
But as for me, I know that my Vindicator lives,
  and that he will at last stand forth upon the dust;
Whom I myself shall see:
  my own eyes, not another's, shall behold him;
And from my flesh I shall see God;
  my inmost being is consumed with longing.

The word of the Lord.

Background of the Reading

Here Job professes faith in God's care for him. Once blessed by God, Job suffers a withdrawal of that blessing. God seems absent. His friends ridicule Job's faith. But the living God is his Vindicator and will free Job from his misery. Job will see the living God, whom he believes longs for him as much as he longs for God. This reading expresses faith in the living God, God's union with your loved one, and his or her desire for eternal union with God.

You might select this reading because your loved one • • •

possessed a faith that rested in God, despite hardships endured • saw the mighty works of God • had great faith in God and longed to see him.

If you select this reading, you might also consider • • •

Psalm 122:1–2, 4–5, 6–7, 8–9 **(RP–8)** • 2 Corinthians 4:14—5:1 **(SR–9)** • John 11:32–45 **(G–15)**

FR–3

As sacrificial offerings he took them to himself.

A reading from the Book of Wisdom

Long form: 3:1-9 [*Short form: 3:1-6, 9*]

[The souls of the just are in the hand of God,
   and no torment shall touch them.
They seemed, in the view of the foolish, to be dead;
   and their passing away was thought an affliction
   and their going forth from us, utter destruction.
But they are in peace.
For if before men, indeed they be punished,
   yet is their hope full of immortality;
Chastised a little, they shall be greatly blessed,
   because God tried them
   and found them worthy of himself.
As gold in the furnace, he proved them,
   and as sacrificial offerings he took them to himself.]
In the time of their visitation they shall shine,
   and shall dart about as sparks through stubble;
They shall judge nations and rule over peoples,
   and the Lord shall be their King forever.
Those who trust in him shall understand truth,
   and the faithful shall abide with him in love:
[Because grace and mercy are with his holy ones,
   and his care is with his elect.]

The word of the Lord.

Background of the Reading

The Book of Wisdom emphasizes that by living justly one is in right relationship with God. The word, immortality, appears for the first time in the Old Testament here. Right relationship leads to an immortal life of peace. Earthly trials are really a discipline to help us learn God's ways as his chosen ones. This reading expresses hope that your loved one shares in the immortality and peace that God offers us.

You might select this reading because your loved one . . .

lived justly, looking out for the welfare of others • admirably dealt with the trials of life • will be greatly missed because of how he or she lived out virtues.

If you select this reading, you might also consider . . .

Psalm 116:5, 6, 10–11, 15–16ac (**RP–7**) • Romans 5:5–11 (**SR–1**) • Luke 23:33, 39–43 (**G–8**)

An unsullied life, the attainment of old age.

A reading from the Book of Wisdom   *4:7–15*

The just man, though he
 die early,
 shall be at rest.
For the age that is honorable
 comes not
 with the passing of time,
 nor can it be measured in
 terms of years.
Rather, understanding is the
 hoary crown for men,
and an unsullied life, the
 attainment of old age.
He who pleased God was loved;
 he who lived among sinners
 was transported—
Snatched away, lest wickedness
 pervert his mind
 or deceit beguile his soul;

For the witchery of paltry things
 obscures what is right
 and the whirl of desire
 transforms the
 innocent mind.
Having become perfect in
 a short while,
he reached the fullness of
 a long career;
for his soul was pleasing
 to the Lord,
therefore he sped him out of
 the midst of wickedness.
But the people saw and did
 not understand,
nor did they take this
 into account.

The word of the Lord.

Background of the Reading

These words correct a false notion that only the wicked die young. The author suggests that those who die at a young age are being preserved from the wickedness and evil that can destroy us. There is still pain when someone dies "before one's time." This reading reiterates the reason to hope that someone who dies at a young age or earlier than we would wish was pleasing to the Lord.

You might select this reading because your loved one • • •

was a young person who had led a good life • was an honorable person who lived only until middle age or less • was a person who has made an impression on the community through a short, well-lived life.

If you select this reading, you might also consider • • •

Psalm 42:2, 3, 5cdef; 43:3, 4, 5 (**RP–4**) • 1 Corinthians 15:51–57 (**SR–8**) • Matthew 25:1–13 (**G–3**)

FR–5

He will destroy death forever.

A reading from the Book of the Prophet Isaiah *25:6a, 7–9*

On this mountain the Lord of hosts
  will provide for all peoples.
On this mountain he will destroy
  the veil that veils all peoples,
The web that is woven over all nations;
  he will destroy death forever.
The Lord God will wipe away
  the tears from all faces;
The reproach of his people he will remove
  from the whole earth; for the Lord has spoken.

  On that day it will be said:
"Behold our God, to whom we looked to save us!
  This is the Lord for whom we looked;
  let us rejoice and be glad that he has saved us!"

The word of the Lord.

Background of the Reading

These words from the first section of the prophet Isaiah are a hymn of thanksgiving for God's saving love. The opening words refer to the heavenly banquet, where God will provide food, joy, reconciliation, and the vision of God forever. It invites us to rejoice and be glad in that saving love. This reading reflects the life of a strong believer, regular communicant, and someone whose long life offers trust that he or she will live in God's peaceful presence for eternity.

You might select this reading when the family of the loved one ● ● ●
needs the consolation of knowing that God is present in their sorrow ●
will be comforted with the knowledge that their loved one is redeemed ●
needs to be assured that we rejoice because God has saved us.

If you select this reading, you might also consider ● ● ●
Psalm 103:8 and 10, 13–14, 15–16, 17–18 **(RP–6)** ● Romans 5:17–21 **(SR–2)** ●
Matthew 11:25–30 **(G–2)**

......

FR–6

It is good to hope in silence for the saving help of the Lord.

A reading from the Book of Lamentations   *3:17–26*

My soul is deprived of peace,
  I have forgotten what
    happiness is;
I tell myself my future is lost,
  all that I hoped for
    from the LORD.
The thought of my
    homeless poverty
  is wormwood and gall;
Remembering it over and
    over leaves my soul
    downcast within me.
But I will call this to mind,
  as my reason to have hope:

The favors of the LORD are
    not exhausted,
  his mercies are not spent;
They are renewed
    each morning,
  so great is his faithfulness.
My portion is the LORD,
    says my soul;
  therefore will I hope in him.

Good is the LORD to one who
    waits for him,
  to the soul that seeks him;
It is good to hope in silence
  for the saving help of the LORD.

The word of the Lord.

Background of the Reading

Lamentations is a book of dirges that recount the sufferings of God's people. The first verses of this reading are part of a litany that names some of those sufferings: lack of peace, forgotten happiness, a lost future, homelessness, and constant anxiety. But then comes our reason to hope: God is with us. Seek the Lord! This reading helps one remember God's nearness and rekindles hope in his saving love for someone who may doubt these realities.

You might select this reading when the family of the loved one . . .
needs to hear that the Lord is merciful • will draw comfort from the knowledge that God is faithful • will find consolation that there is always hope in God.

If you select this reading, you might also consider . . .
Psalm 27:1, 4, 7 and 8b and 9a, 13–14 (**RP–3**) • Romans 14:7–9, 10c–12 (**SR–6**) • Matthew 25:31–46 (**G–4**)

FR–7

Many of those who sleep in the dust of the earth shall awake.

A reading from the Book of the Prophet Daniel *12:1-3*

In those days,
   I, Daniel, mourned
and heard this word
   of the Lord:
At that time there shall arise
   Michael, the great prince,
   guardian of your people;
It shall be a time unsurpassed
   in distress
   since nations began until
   that time.
At that time your people
   shall escape,
   everyone who is found
   written in the book.

Many of those who sleep in
   the dust of the earth
   shall awake;
Some shall live forever,
   others shall be an everlasting
   horror and disgrace.
But the wise shall shine brightly
   like the splendor of
   the firmament,
And those who lead the
   many to justice
   shall be like the stars forever.

The word of the Lord.

Background of the Reading

The Book of Daniel is apocalyptic writing—that is, about the end of time. These verses offer hope after predictions of disaster and crises. They give us the first statement in the Scriptures about belief in the resurrection of the dead and life everlasting. This reading can reiterate your hope and ours, that your loved one will awake and shine like the stars forever because of God's merciful love.

You might select this reading because your loved one • • •
was considered wise • had a faith that emanated to others • was a leader who guided others in the faith.

If you select this reading, you might also consider • • •
Psalm 23:1–3, 4, 5, 6 **(RP–1)** • Romans 8:31b–35, 37–39 **(SR–5)** •
Luke 23:44–46, 50, 52–53; 24:1–6a or 23:44–46, 50–53 **(G–9)**

The First Reading from the New Testament during Easter Time

When a Catholic funeral is celebrated during Easter Time, the First Reading comes from the New Testament Acts of the Apostles or the Book of Revelation. There are four options for readings during Easter Time, found in this chapter numbered **FRE–1**, **FRE–2**, and so on.

Some of these readings may sound familiar to you, while others may not. Read each passage carefully. Choose the reading that best speaks about your loved one's life, your faith, and faith in the death and Resurrection of Christ, as you gather to prepare the funeral liturgy.

If the funeral of your loved one takes place outside of Easter Time, refer to the First Reading options beginning on page 1.

If you are not sure what reading to choose, your pastor or whomever you are meeting with to prepare the funeral can help.

FRE–1

He is the one appointed by God as judge of the living and the dead.

A reading from the Acts of the Apostles

Long form: 10:34–43 [*Short form: 10:34–36, 42–43*]

[Peter proceeded to speak, saying:
"In truth, I see that God shows no partiality.
Rather, in every nation whoever fears him and acts uprightly
is acceptable to him.
You know the word that he sent to the children of Israel
as he proclaimed peace through Jesus Christ, who is Lord of all,]
what has happened all over Judea,
beginning in Galilee after the baptism
that John preached,
how God anointed Jesus of Nazareth
with the Holy Spirit and power.
He went about doing good
and healing all those oppressed by the Devil,
for God was with him.
We are witnesses of all that he did
both in the country of the Jews and in Jerusalem.
They put him to death by hanging him on a tree.
This man God raised on the third day and granted that he be visible,
not to all the people, but to us,
the witnesses chosen by God in advance,
who ate and drank with him after he rose from the dead.
[He commissioned us to preach to the people
and testify that he is the one appointed by God
as judge of the living and the dead.
To him all the prophets bear witness,
that everyone who believes in him
will receive forgiveness of sins through his name."]

The word of the Lord.

Background of the Reading

Acts of the Apostles was written by the evangelist Luke and tells the story of the growth of the early Church inspired by the Holy Spirit. This passage, a preaching by St. Peter, presents the basic teaching about Jesus' life, death, Resurrection, and his sending the Apostles to preach God's mercy to all people, by means of their words and deeds. It reminds us that God shows no partiality, and anyone whose words and deeds helped others see Jesus can experience God's saving love.

You might select this reading because your loved one . . .

was strengthened by participation in the Eucharist • did not fear witnessing to his or her faith • preached through a life that was close to the Church and the sacraments.

If you select this reading, you might also consider . . .

Psalm 103:8 and 10, 13–14, 15–16, 17–18 **(RP–6)** • 2 Timothy 2:8–13 **(SR–13)** • John 6:37–40 **(G–12)**

．．．．．．

FRE–2

Blessed are the dead who die in the Lord.

A reading from the Book of Revelation   *14:13*

I, John, heard a voice from heaven say, "Write this:
   Blessed are the dead who die in the Lord from now on."
"Yes," said the Spirit,
   "let them find rest from their labors,
   for their works accompany them."

The word of the Lord.

Background of the Reading

Revelation, written by the author of John's account of the Gospel, offers a picture of the end of time. In this reading, John gives us a new beatitude: Those who die in the Lord are blessed and will find rest, because their works go with them. We live the way of Jesus as a sign of faith, not to earn it. Faith is a gift and can't be earned. This reading reminds us that people who lived their faith in clear and concrete ways are blessed and model for mourners how to live their faith too.

You might select this reading because your loved one ● ● ●
tirelessly advocated for the faith ● practiced the spiritual and corporal works of mercy ● lived out the faith through selfless acts.

If you select this reading, you might also consider ● ● ●
Psalm 42:2, 3, 5cdef; 43:3, 4, 5 **(RP–4)** ● 1 Corinthians 15:51–57 **(SR–8)** ● Matthew 25:1–13 **(G–3)**

FRE–3

The dead were judged according to their deeds.

A reading from the Book of Revelation   20:11—21:1

I, John, saw a large white
   throne and the one who
   was sitting on it.
The earth and the sky fled
   from his presence
and there was no place for them.
I saw the dead, the great
   and the lowly, standing
   before the throne,
and scrolls were opened.
Then another scroll was opened,
   the book of life.
The dead were judged
   according to their deeds,
by what was written
   in the scrolls.
The sea gave up its dead;
   then Death and Hades
      gave up their dead.

All the dead were judged
   according to their deeds.
Then Death and Hades were
   thrown into the pool of fire.
(This pool of fire is the
   second death.)
Anyone whose name was
   not found written in
   the book of life
was thrown into the pool
   of fire.

Then I saw a new heaven
   and a new earth.
The former heaven and
   the former earth had
   passed away,
and the sea was no more.

The word of the Lord.

Background of the Reading

Revelation paints a mysterious picture about God's self-manifestation at the end of time. The writer, John, portrays God seated on a white throne and ushering in a new heaven and a new earth. Death and sin are no more. Our deeds determine whether or not we are destined for eternal life. Found there, we will live with God forever. This reading reminds mourners that they still have time to choose God's ways. It offers hope that your loved one will be part of the new heaven and earth.

You might select this reading because your loved one . . .
was known for their righteous deeds • lived an exemplary life • acted on behalf of others.

If you select this reading, you might also consider . . .
Psalm 42:2, 3, 5cdef; 43:3, 4, 5 (**RP-4**) • Romans 6:3–9 or 6:3–4, 8–9 (**SR-3**) • Matthew 25:1–13 (**G-3**)

FRE–4

There shall be no more death.

A reading from the Book of Revelation   *21:1–5a, 6b–7*

I, John, saw a new heaven
    and a new earth.
The former heaven and the former
    earth had passed away,
and the sea was no more.
I also saw the holy city,
    a new Jerusalem,
coming down out of
    heaven from God,
prepared as a bride adorned
    for her husband.
I heard a loud voice from
    the throne saying,
"Behold, God's dwelling is
    with the human race.
He will dwell with them and they
    will be his people
and God himself will always be
    with them as their God.

He will wipe every tear from
    their eyes,
and there shall be no more death
    or mourning,
      wailing or pain,
for the old order has passed away."

The One who sat on the
    throne said,
  "Behold, I make all things new."
I am the Alpha and the Omega,
    the beginning and the end.
To the thirsty I will give a gift
    from the spring
      of life-giving water.
The victor will inherit these gifts,
    and I shall be his God,
    and he will be my son."

The word of the Lord.

Background of the Reading

In this climactic scene about the end times, the writer, John, clarifies God's reign. Jerusalem descends from heaven to earth. God dwells with the human race and removes fear, tears, death, and mourning. God speaks to us: "Behold, I make all things new," fulfilling God's promise to dwell with us forever as his sons and daughters. What words of hope, especially for one whose life was filled with pain and suffering and for those gathered in tears who seek comfort and joy!

You might select this reading because your loved one . . .
experienced much pain • suffered through a long illness • endured a life with many hardships.

If you select this reading, you might also consider . . .
Psalm 122:1–2, 4–5, 6–7, 8–9 **(RP–8)** • 2 Corinthians 4:14—5:1 **(SR–9)** • John 11:32–45 **(G–15)**

The Responsorial Psalm

Following the First Reading at Catholic funerals, we sing (preferred) or say the Responsorial Psalm. Singing is preferred because most psalms were written as sung poems. Found in the Old Testament Book of Psalms, they reflect almost every human emotion, from hope to sorrow. They powerfully express suffering, pain, hope, and trust of people of all ages and cultures. They sing our faith in God. The psalms help all who gather put the words of Scripture on their lips, like Jesus did when he prayed them.

The psalms help mourners express their feelings at a funeral and they can reflect our loved one's life. They are called "responsorial" because they are prayed alternating between psalmist (the person who sings or says the psalm) and people, and because they can reflect a sentiment in the First Reading.

There are ten options for the funeral of an adult, found in this chapter numbered **RP–1**, **RP–2**, and so on. While some psalms are familiar, pray through all the options. Discover which one helps you express your feelings in light of faith. Meet with your parish musician to select a sung setting of the chosen psalm.

RP–1 *Psalm 23:1–3, 4, 5, 6 (1 or 4ab)*

R. The Lord is my shepherd; there is nothing I shall want.
 or:
R. Though I walk in the valley of darkness, I fear no evil,
 for you are with me.

The LORD is my shepherd;
 I shall not want.
In verdant pastures
 he gives me repose;
Beside restful waters he leads me;
 he refreshes my soul.
He guides me in right paths
 for his name's sake. **R.**

Even though I walk in
 the dark valley
I fear no evil;
 for you are at my side
With your rod and your staff
 that give me courage. **R.**

You spread the table before me
 in the sight of my foes;
You anoint my head with oil;
 my cup overflows. **R.**

Only goodness and kindness
 follow me
all the days of my life;
And I shall dwell in the house
 of the LORD
 for years to come. **R.**

Background of the Reading

Most people are familiar with Psalm 23 or know it by heart. God is a shepherd, a frequent Old Testament image, who offers trust, rest, refreshment, guidance, and protection. Verses 5 and 6 express God's abundant hospitality, offering food, protection, kindness, and an eternal dwelling. Sing Psalm 23 to express someone's trust in God, care for others, graciousness (refrain 1), or for one who needs rest and peace after a difficult life (refrain 2).

You might select this psalm when the family of the loved one • • •
will draw comfort from hearing that God will be present to them • finds solace in hearing that God will lead them through their sorrow • needs to feel that God offers a refuge for them.

If you select this reading, you might also consider • • •
Daniel 12:1–3 (**FR–7**) • Revelation 20:11—21:1 (**FRE–3**) • Romans 8:31b–35, 37–39 (**SR–5**) • Luke 23:44–46, 50, 52–53; 24:1–6a or 23:44–46, 50–53 (**G–9**)

RP–2 *Psalm 25:6 and 7b, 17–18, 20–21 (1 or 3a)*

R. To you, O Lord, I lift my soul.
or:
R. No one who waits for you, O Lord, will ever be put to shame.

Remember that your compassion, O Lᴏʀᴅ,
  and your kindness are from of old.
In your kindness remember me,
  because of your goodness, O Lᴏʀᴅ. **R.**

Relieve the troubles of my heart;
  and bring me out of my distress.
Put an end to my affliction and my suffering;
  and take away all my sins. **R.**

Preserve my life and rescue me;
  let me not be put to shame, for I take refuge in you.
Let integrity and uprightness preserve me,
  because I wait for you, O Lᴏʀᴅ. **R.**

Background of the Reading

Psalm 24 is a song of lament. With one exception, each verse begins with a different letter of the Hebrew alphabet. This structure is a statement that all life, from beginning to end, leads to God. Verses 17–21 plead directly to God for relief from suffering and shame. Verses 6 and 7b ask for God's compassion and kindness. Choose refrain 1 as a prayer of submission to God's merciful love and refrain 2 to express trust that God will remember compassion from of old.

You might select this psalm because your loved one • • •
lived with integrity • suffered greatly • underwent much distress.

If you select this reading, you might also consider • • •
Job 19:1, 23–27a **(FR–2)** • Acts 10:34–43 or 10:34–36, 42–43 **(FRE–1)** •
2 Timothy 2:8–13 **(SR–13)** • Matthew 5:1–12a **(G–1)**

RP–3 *Psalm 27:1, 4, 7 and 8b and 9a, 13–14 (1a or 13)*

R. The Lord is my light and my salvation.
   or:
R. I believe that I shall see the good things
   of the Lord in the land of the living.

The Lord is my light and
      my salvation;
   whom should I fear?
The Lord is my life's refuge;
   of whom should
         I be afraid? **R.**

One thing I ask of the Lord;
   this I seek:
To dwell in the house of the Lord
   all the days of my life,
That I may gaze on the
      loveliness of the Lord
   and contemplate
         his temple. **R.**

Hear, O Lord,
      the sound of my call;
   have pity on me,
      and answer me.
Your presence, O Lord, I seek.
   Hide not your face from me. **R.**

I believe that I shall see the
      bounty of the Lord
   in the land of the living.
Wait for the Lord with courage;
   be stouthearted, and wait for
      the Lord. **R.**

Background of the Reading

Psalm 27 is a hymn of trust in God at all times, including desperation. Verses 1–6 are a prayer of confidence, and 7–14, a prayer of lament. God's light is stronger than any darkness. So seek that light and wait for the Lord. You will dwell with God forever. Refrain 2 is a statement of faith that your loved one will dwell in the land of the living. Refrain 1 expresses hope in God's guiding light. Both refrains proclaim that you believe in God's promises, as did your loved one.

You might select this psalm because your loved one • • •

was a person of prayer who sought God in creation • was a faithful person who found refuge in God • was a person of prayer.

If you select this reading, you might also consider • • •

2 Maccabees 12:43–46 (**FR–1**) • Revelation 20:11—21:1 (**FRE–3**) • Romans 6:3–9 or 6:3–4, 8–9 (**SR–3**) • Matthew 25:1–13 (**G–3**)

RP–4   *Psalm 42:2, 3, 5cdef; 43:3, 4, 5 (42:3)*

**R. My soul is thirsting for the living God:
when shall I see him face to face?**

As the hind longs for the
    running waters,
so my soul longs for you,
    O God. **R.**

Athirst is my soul for God,
    the living God.
When shall I go and behold
    the face of God? **R.**

I went with the throng and
    led them in procession
to the house of God.
Amid loud cries of joy
    and thanksgiving,
with the multitude
    keeping festival. **R.**

Send forth your light and
    your fidelity;
they shall lead me on
And bring me to your
    holy mountain,
to your dwelling-place. **R.**

Then will I go in to the altar of God,
    the God of my gladness and joy;
Then will I give you thanks
    upon the harp,
    O God, my God! **R.**

Why are you so downcast,
    O my soul?
    Why do you sigh within me?
Hope in God! For I shall again
    be thanking him,
    in the presence of my savior
    and my God. **R.**

Background of the Reading

Psalm 42 exudes human longing for God based on earlier experiences of union with God. The psalmist asks for the light and faithfulness that lead to God's holy mountain, where we will worship at God's altar. The concluding verses encourage hope that sorrow will end and the promised resurrection will occur. The refrain expresses human longing to see God face to face and our desire to be reunited with our loved one in his presence forever.

You might select this psalm because your loved one • • •
was thankful for all God has done • looked to God for guidance • desired union with God.

If you select this reading, you might also consider • • •
Wisdom 4:7–15 **(FR–4)** • Revelation 14:13 **(FRE–2)** • 1 Corinthians 15:51–57 **(SR–8)** • Matthew 25:1–13 **(G–3)**

RP–5   *Psalm 63:2, 3–4, 5–6, 8–9 (2b)*

R. My soul is thirsting for you, O Lord my God.

O God, you are my God whom I seek;
   for you my flesh pines and my soul thirsts
   like the earth, parched, lifeless and without water. **R.**

Thus have I gazed toward you in the sanctuary
   to see your power and your glory,
For your kindness is a greater good than life;
   my lips shall glorify you. **R.**

Thus will I bless you while I live;
   lifting up my hands, I will call upon your name.
As with the riches of a banquet shall my soul be satisfied,
   and with exultant lips my mouth shall praise you. **R.**

You are my help,
   and in the shadow of your wings I shout for joy.
My soul clings fast to you;
   your right hand upholds me. **R.**

Background of the Reading

The refrain and opening verses of Psalm 63 express human longing
for God, even when one feels parched and dry. This is a prayer of confident thanksgiving for God's generous love. It professes faith that life
does not end in physical death. Psalm 63 can voice your loved one's
belief in God and the promise of resurrection. It can also help you take
comfort in the fact that, since God's hand upholds us, life is changed,
not ended.

You might select this psalm because your loved one • • •
had great reverence for God • sought God's help during adversity • blessed
God's name during joyous and difficult times.

If you select this reading, you might also consider • • •
Wisdom 3:1–9 or 3:1–6, 9 **(FR–3)** • Acts 10:34–43 or 10:34–36, 42–43
(FRE–1) • Romans 8:14–23 **(SR–4)** • John 11:17–27 or 11:21–27 **(G–14)**

Psalm 103:8 and 10, 13–14, 15–16, 17–18 (8a or 37:39a)

R. The Lord is kind and merciful.
or:
R. The salvation of the just comes from the Lord.

Merciful and gracious is the LORD,
  slow to anger, and abounding
    in kindness.
Not according to our sins does
  he deal with us,
  nor does he requite us according
    to our crimes. **R.**

Man's days are like those of grass;
  like a flower of the field
    he blooms;
The wind sweeps over him
    and he is gone,
  and his place knows him
    no more. **R.**

As a father has compassion
  on his children,
so the LORD has compassion on
    those who fear him.
For he knows how we are formed,
  he remembers that
    we are dust. **R.**

But the kindness of the LORD
    is from eternity,
  to eternity toward those
    who fear him,
And his justice toward
    children's children
  among those who keep
    his covenant
and remember to fulfill his
    precepts. **R.**

Background of the Reading

Psalm 103 is a creedal hymn expressing faith in God's unconditional love and mercy. The verses clarify that God's mercy is offered in the face of human sin and weakness. Even there, God abounds in kindness, like a compassionate parent. God remembers us after human memory fails. Refrain 1 reinforces God's merciful nature. Refrain 2 affirms God's love in the face of sin. Choose this psalm for someone who doubted God's mercy and to reinforce trust.

You might select this psalm when the family of the loved one • • •
needs to feel God's compassion for their loved one • will find comfort in God's kindness • will draw consolation from hearing of God's mercy.

If you select this reading, you might also consider • • •
Isaiah 25:6a, 7–9 **(FR–5)** • Acts 10:34–43 or 10:34–36, 42–43 **(FRE–1)** • 2 Timothy 2:8–13 **(SR–13)** • John 6:37–40 **(G–12)**

RP–7   *Psalm 116:5, 6, 10–11, 15–16ac (9)*

R. I will walk in the presence of the Lord in the land of the living.
  or:
R. Alleluia.

Gracious is the LORD and just;
  yes, our God is merciful. **R.**

The LORD keeps the little ones;
  I was brought low, and he saved me. **R.**

I believed, even when I said,
  "I am greatly afflicted";
I said in my alarm
  "No man is dependable." **R.**

Precious in the eyes of the LORD
  is the death of his faithful ones.
O LORD, I am your servant,
  you have loosed my bonds. **R.**

Background of the Reading

The psalmist gives praise and thanks to God for being gracious and merciful to the faithful servant who was saved, even when greatly afflicted. God is dependable when human beings are not. Refrain 1 proclaims confident trust: "I will walk in the presence of the Lord in the land of the living." Why? Because your loved one, and all gathered to honor her or his life, is precious in God's eyes. Refrain 2 expresses the joy of that fact in the familiar, untranslatable, word, *Alleluia*!

You might select this psalm because your loved one • • •
had a strong belief in God • possessed a deep faith • was involved in ministry in the Church and considered his or her work to be that of a servant.

If you select this reading, you might also consider • • •
•Wisdom 3:1–9 or 3:1–6, 9 **(FR–3)** • Acts 10:34–43 or 10:34–36, 42–43 **(FRE–1)** • Romans 5:5–11 **(SR–1)** • Luke 23:33, 39–43 **(G–8)**

RP–8 *Psalm 122:1–2, 4–5, 6–7, 8–9 (1 or see 1)*

R. I rejoiced when I heard them say: let us go to the house of the Lord.
or:
R. Let us go rejoicing to the house of the Lord.

I rejoiced because they
    said to me,
"We will go up to the house
    of the Lord."
And now we have set foot
    within your gates,
      O Jerusalem. **R.**

To it the tribes go up,
    the tribes of the Lord.
According to the decree for Israel,
    to give thanks to the name of
      the Lord.
In it are set up judgment seats,
    seats for the house of David. **R.**

Pray for the peace of Jerusalem!
    May those who love you prosper!
May peace be within your walls,
    prosperity in your buildings. **R.**

Because of my relatives
    and friends
I will say "Peace be within you!"
Because of the house of the Lord,
    our God,
I will pray for your good. **R.**

Background of the Reading

Psalm 122 is a "Song of Zion," Jerusalem, the city of peace, where God dwells with his people. This pilgrimage psalm is sung on the journey through death to the house of the Lord in Jerusalem. In this psalm of trust and hope, we pray for the peace of our relatives and friends, and ask them to pray for us. Both refrains express joy for being at this stage of one's journey home. And both refrains invite us to rejoice, no matter where we are on life's journey.

You might select this psalm because your loved one • • •
focused his or her life on God • gave thanks to God • worked for peace in the home or community.

If you select this reading, you might also consider • • •
Job 19:1, 23–27a **(FR–2)** • Revelation 21:1–5a, 6b–7 **(FRE–4)** •
2 Corinthians 4:14—5:1 **(SR–9)** • John 11:32–45 **(G–15)**

RP–9 *Psalm 130:1–2, 3–4, 5–6ab, 6c–7, 8 (1 or see 50)*

R. Out of the depths, I cry to you, Lord.
or:
R. I hope in the Lord, I trust in his word.

Out of the depths I cry to you,
O Lord;
Lord, hear my voice!
Let your ears be attentive
to my voice in supplication. **R.**

If you, O Lord, mark iniquities,
Lord, who can stand?
But with you is forgiveness,
that you may be revered. **R.**

I trust in the Lord;
my soul trusts in his word.
My soul waits for the Lord
more than the sentinels wait
for the dawn. **R.**

More than the sentinels wait
for the dawn,
let Israel wait for the Lord,
For with the Lord is kindness
and with him is plenteous
redemption. **R.**

And he will redeem Israel
from all their iniquities. **R.**

Background of the Reading

Psalm 130 is a hymn of lament. We can feel the angst of someone weighed down by sin. Verses 1–4 are addressed directly to our all-powerful and merciful God. Verses 5–9, addressed to the community, express trust in God's redeeming love, hope in God's mercy, and humble admission that we need both. Refrain 1 expresses how overwhelming sinfulness can feel. Refrain 2 proclaims that no matter when we turn to God we will be all right, we have reason to hope.

You might select this psalm because your loved one . . .
lived trusting God • was sick for a long time • lived with gratitude for all God has done.

If you select this reading, you might also consider . . .
Isaiah 25:6a, 7–9 **(FR–5)** • Revelation 21:1–5a, 6b–7 **(FRE–4)** • Philippians 3:20–21 **(SR–11)** • Luke 12:35–40 **(G–7)**

RP–10 *Psalm 143:1–2, 5–6, 7ab and 8ab, 10 (1a)*

R. O Lord, hear my prayer.

O Lord, hear my prayer;
  hearken to my pleading in your faithfulness;
  in your justice answer me.
And enter not into judgment with your servant,
  for before you no living man is just. **R.**

I remember the days of old;
  I meditate on all your doings;
  the works of your hands I ponder.
I stretch out my hands to you;
  my soul thirsts for you like parched land. **R.**

Hasten to answer me, O Lord;
  for my spirit fails me.
At dawn let me hear of your mercy,
  for in you I trust. **R.**

Teach me to do your will,
  for you are my God.
May your good spirit guide me
  on level ground. **R.**

Background of the Reading

Like Psalm 130 (see page 26), Psalm 143 is a hymn of lament. It opens by affirming God's faithfulness and admitting one's sinfulness. Next the psalmist recalls God's saving acts, and, with arms outstretched in surrender and need, throws oneself on God's mercy. Finally, we ask God to answer this prayer quickly with mercy and guidance. This psalm reflects the fact that all of us are utterly dependent upon God and seek his will here and in the hereafter.

You might select this psalm because your loved one . . .
understood our dependence on God's mercy • looked to God for guidance • considered God to be just.

If you select this reading, you might also consider . . .
Lamentations 3:17–26 **(FR–6)** • Revelation 14:13 **(FRE–2)** • 2 Corinthians 5:1, 6–10 **(SR–10)** • Mark 15:33–39; 16:1–6 or 15:33–39 **(G–5)**

The Second Reading from the New Testament

The Second Reading at a Catholic funeral comes from the New Testament letters of Saint Paul or Saint John. There are fifteen options from which to choose, found in this chapter numbered **SR–1**, **SR–2**, and so on. The readings proclaim that we share in Christ's death and Resurrection by virtue of our Baptism.

We hear many of these selections at Sunday Mass during Easter Time and so they may be familiar to you already. The Scripture passages provide words of hope and compassion that call us to trust, for having died with Christ, we shall rise with him. Keep that in mind as you read and reflect on the Scripture passages. Select the reading that connects you with your loved one and how he or she shares in Christ's victory over death.

If you are not sure what reading to choose, your pastor or whomever you are meeting with to prepare the funeral can help.

SR–1

Since we are now justified by his Blood, we will be saved through him from the wrath.

A reading from the Letter of Saint Paul to the Romans   *5:5–11*

Brothers and sisters:
Hope does not disappoint,
    because the love of God has been
        poured out into our hearts
    through the Holy Spirit who has
        been given to us.
For Christ, while we were
        still helpless,
    died at the appointed time
        for the ungodly.
Indeed, only with difficulty does
        one die for a just person,
    though perhaps for a good person
    one might even find courage
        to die.
But God proves his love for us
    in that while we were still
        sinners Christ died for us.

How much more then,
        since we are now justified
        by his Blood,
    will we be saved through him
        from the wrath.
Indeed, if, while we were enemies,
    we were reconciled to God
        through the death of his Son,
    how much more, once reconciled,
    will we be saved by his life.
Not only that,
    but we also boast of God through
        our Lord Jesus Christ,
    through whom we have now
        received reconciliation.

The word of the Lord.

Background of the Reading

Paul's letter to the Romans affirms God's unconditional gift of love, through the Holy Spirit given to us. That gift was offered to us by Jesus' total gift of self through his death on the Cross. Christ's death restored the relationship with God that was lost by sin. Since Christ died for all, both those who were faithful to God and those who were not, we can hope that our loved one will be with God forever. That is our hope, too.

You might select this reading because your loved one . . .
believed in the redemptive mercy of God • lived with hope • anticipated being saved by God's reconciling love.

If you select this reading, you might also consider . . .
Wisdom 3:1–9 or 3:1–6, 9 **(FR–3)** • Acts 10:34–43 or 10:34–36, 42–43 **(FRE–1)** • Psalm 116:5, 6, 10–11, 15–16ac **(RP–7)** • Luke 23:33, 39–43 **(G–8)**

······

SR–2

Where sin increased, grace overflowed all the more.

A reading from the Letter of Saint Paul to the Romans   *5:17–21*

Brothers and sisters:
If, by the transgression of the one,
  death came to reign through
    that one,
  how much more will those
    who receive the abundance
    of grace
and of the gift of justification
come to reign in life through the
    one Jesus Christ.
In conclusion, just as through
    one transgression
  condemnation came upon all,
so, through one righteous act,
  acquittal and life came to all.
For just as through the
    disobedience of the one man
  the many were made sinners,
  so through the obedience
    of the one
  the many will be made righteous.
The law entered in so
    that transgression
    might increase
but, where sin increased, grace
    overflowed all the more,
    so that,
as sin reigned in death,
grace also might reign through
    justification for eternal life
  through Jesus Christ our Lord.

The word of the Lord.

Background of the Reading

This selection from Romans can be summarized like this: God's very life and grace is greater than any sin we can commit. Jesus was obedient to living God's will in the face of rejection, suffering, and death on the Cross. His obedience restored our relationship with God and made it possible for us to share eternal life. No amount of sin could stop God's generous love made visible in Christ Jesus. These are words of confident hope.

You might select this reading because your loved one ● ● ●
knew he or she was dependent on God's grace ● looked to God to be made righteous ● had faith in the mercy of God.

If you select this reading, you might also consider ● ● ●
Isaiah 25:6a, 7–9 **(FR–5)** ● Revelation 21:1–5a, 6b–7 **(FRE–4)** ● Psalm 103:8 and 10, 13–14, 15–16, 17–18 **(RP–6)** ● Matthew 11:25–30 **(G–2)**

SR–3

We too might live in newness of life.

A reading from the Letter of Saint Paul to the Romans

Long form: 6:3-9 [*Short form: 6:3-4, 8-9*]

[Brothers and sisters:
Are you unaware that we who were
    baptized into Christ Jesus
were baptized into his death?
We were indeed buried with him
    through baptism into death,
so that, just as Christ was
    raised from the dead
by the glory of the Father,
we too might live in
    newness of life.]

For if we have grown into
    union with him through
    a death like his,
we shall also be united with
    him in the resurrection.

We know that our old self was
    crucified with him,
so that our sinful body might
    be done away with,
that we might no longer be
    in slavery to sin.
For a dead person has been
    absolved from sin.
[If, then, we have died with Christ,
    we believe that we shall also
    live with him.
We know that Christ, raised from
    the dead, dies no more;
death no longer has power
    over him.]

The word of the Lord.

Background of the Reading

Romans 6 proclaims the power of our Baptism, which unites us with
Jesus Christ in a most intimate way. We have died with him, a death
to sin and anything that is not of Christ. Having become one with
Christ through Baptism, we will share in his Resurrection. We will be
made new. We can trust in that promise and celebrate it as we gather
to celebrate a Christian death. Know it! Believe it! Celebrate it!

You might select this reading because your loved one ...

believed that Baptism unites our lives with Christ • held that just as
Jesus was raised from the dead so will we be raised • trusted that God
has power over death.

If you select this reading, you might also consider ...

2 Maccabees 12:43–46 **(FR–1)** • Revelation 20:11—21:1 **(FRE–3)** •
Psalm 42:2, 3, 5cdef; 43:3, 4, 5 **(RP–4)** • Matthew 25:1–13 **(G–3)**

SR–4

We also groan within ourselves as we wait for adoption, the redemption of our bodies.

A reading from the Letter of Saint Paul to the Romans   *8:14–23*

Brothers and sisters:
Those who are led by the Spirit of God are sons of God.
For you did not receive a spirit of slavery to fall back into fear,
  but you received a spirit of adoption,
  through which we cry, *"Abba*, Father!"
The Spirit itself bears witness with our spirit
  that we are children of God,
  and if children, then heirs,
  heirs of God and joint heirs with Christ,
  if only we suffer with him
  so that we may also be glorified with him.

I consider that the sufferings of this present time are as nothing
  compared with the glory to be revealed for us.
For creation awaits with eager expectation
  the revelation of the children of God;
  for creation was made subject to futility,
  not of its own accord but because of the one who subjected it,
  in hope that creation itself
  would be set free from slavery to corruption
  and share in the glorious freedom of the children of God.
We know that all creation is groaning in labor pains even until now;
  and not only that, but we ourselves,
  who have the first fruits of the Spirit,
  we also groan within ourselves
  as we wait for adoption, the redemption of our bodies.

The word of the Lord.

Background of the Reading

This reading makes clear how receiving the Holy Spirit changes our relationship with God. The Spirit makes us adopted children, members of God's family. We can call God, "Abba," daddy! A slave is not an heir but a child is. United with Christ, we become heirs to life with God. Suffering, especially the discipline of living our faith, gives us a share in new life, like the pain of childbirth gives birth to a child. United with Christ, death gives birth to resurrection.

You might select this reading when the family of the loved one . . .
will draw comfort from hearing their loved one called a child of God • will be consoled by the word *Abba*, the word that Jesus used for Father • will find solace in hearing that those who suffer with Christ are also glorified in him.

If you select this reading, you might also consider . . .
Wisdom 3:1–9 or 3:1–6, 9 **(FR–3)** • Revelation 14:13 **(FRE–2)** • Psalm 63:2, 3–4, 5–6, 8–9 **(RP–5)** • John 6:37–40 **(G–12)**

SR–5

What will separate us from the love of Christ!

A reading from the Letter of Saint Paul to the Romans
8:31b–35, 37–39

Brothers and sisters:
If God is for us, who can be against us?
He did not spare his own Son
   but handed him over for us all,
   will he not also give us everything else along with him?
Who will bring a charge against God's chosen ones?
It is God who acquits us.
Who will condemn?
It is Christ Jesus who died, rather, was raised,
   who also is at the right hand of God,
   who indeed intercedes for us.
What will separate us from the love of Christ?
Will anguish, or distress or persecution, or famine,
   or nakedness, or peril, or the sword?

No, in all these things, we conquer overwhelmingly
   through him who loved us.
For I am convinced that neither death, nor life,
   nor angels, nor principalities,
   nor present things, nor future things,
   nor powers, nor height, nor depth,
   nor any other creature will be able to separate us
   from the love of God in Christ Jesus our Lord.

The word of the Lord.

Background of the Reading

This reading is a hymn proclaiming the utter love that God has for us. God *is* for us, so no one or no thing can be against us. Christ died out of love for us, was raised by God the Father, and sits at the Father's right hand to intercede for us. We gather to intercede for our loved one, fully confident that nothing: death, life, angels, powers, the present nor the future, will separate our loved one or us from God's love made visible in Christ Jesus. God *is* for us. Believe it and bank on it.

You might select this reading when the family of the loved one . . .
will find comfort hearing that nothing separates us from Christ's love •
will draw consolation from knowing that Christ intercedes for us •
needs to hear that God always gives us what we need.

If you select this reading, you might also consider . . .
Daniel 12:1–3 **(FR–7)** • Revelation 21:1–5a, 6b–7 **(FRE–4)** • Psalm 23:1–3, 4, 5, 6 **(RP–1)** • Luke 23:44–46, 50, 52–53; 24:1–6a or 23:44–46, 50–53 **(G–9)**

SR–6

Whether we live or die, we are the Lord's.

A reading from the Letter of Saint Paul to the Romans

14:7–9, 10c–12

Brothers and sisters:
No one lives for oneself,
  and no one dies for oneself.
For if we live, we live for the Lord,
  and if we die, we die for the Lord;
  so then, whether we live or die, we are the Lord's.
For this is why Christ died and came to life,
  that he might be Lord of both the dead and the living.
Why then do you judge your brother?
Or you, why do you look down on your brother?
For we shall all stand before the judgment seat of God;
  for it is written:
    As I live, says the Lord, every knee shall bend before me,
      and every tongue shall give praise to God.

So then each of us shall give an accounting of
  himself to God.

The word of the Lord.

Background of the Reading

Those who belong to Christ are so transformed that they live for God, not for themselves. If that is true of life with Christ, it is also true of death with Christ. We die in the Lord. Death, like sin, is the great equalizer. In the end, all will stand before God, so do not judge anyone else. Live in ways that obey and praise God, and you will belong to the Lord when you die.

You might select this reading because your loved one · · ·
was someone who lived for others • was an individual known for doing good works • was a person who lived an honorable life, ready to give an accounting to God.

If you select this reading, you might also consider · · ·
Lamentations 3:17–26 **(FR–6)** • Revelation 14:13 **(FRE–2)** • Psalm 27:1, 4, 7 and 8b and 9a, 13–14 **(RP–3)** • Matthew 25:31–46 **(G–4)**

So too in Christ shall all be brought to life.

A reading from the first Letter of Saint Paul to the Corinthians

Long form: 15:20–28 [Short form: 15:20–23]

[Brothers and sisters:
Christ has been raised from the dead,
  the firstfruits of those who have fallen asleep.
For since death came through a man,
  the resurrection of the dead came also through man.
For just as in Adam all die,
  so too in Christ shall all be brought to life,
  but each one in proper order:
  Christ the firstfruits;
  then, at his coming, those who belong to Christ;]
  then comes the end,
  when he hands over the Kingdom to his God and Father.
For he must reign until he has put all his enemies under his feet.
The last enemy to be destroyed is death,
  for "he subjected everything under his feet."
But when it says that everything has been subjected,
  it is clear that it excludes the one who subjected everything to him.
When everything is subjected to him,
  then the Son himself will also be subjected
  to the one who subjected everything to him,
  so that God may be all in all.

The word of the Lord.

Background of the Reading

One of St. Paul's favorite themes is the comparison between Adam and Christ. In Adam all die. In Christ, the first fruits of those who died, the entire harvest of God's people is dedicated to God. All share in Christ's victory over death, which will be destroyed. All people and all creation can rise and share God's everlasting reign. Trust these words of promise for those we bury, and for those who gather in prayer and thanksgiving, for comfort.

You might select this reading when the family of the loved one . . .
will draw comfort from hearing that all will be brought to life in Christ • will be consoled knowing that all who belong to Christ will rise from the dead • needs to hear that everything, even death, is subjected to Christ.

If you select this reading, you might also consider . . .
Daniel 12:1–3 **(FR–7)** • Acts 10:34–43 or 10:34–36, 42–43 **(FRE–1)** • Psalm 103:8 and 10, 13–14, 15–16, 17–18 **(RP–6)** • Matthew 11:25–30 **(G–2)**

SR–8

Death is swallowed up in victory.

A reading from the first Letter of Saint Paul to the Corinthians
15:51–57

Brothers and sisters:
Behold, I tell you a mystery.
We shall not all fall asleep,
    but we will all be changed,
in an instant, in the blink of
    an eye, at the last trumpet.
For the trumpet will sound,
    the dead will be raised
    incorruptible,
and we shall be changed.
For that which is corruptible
    must clothe itself
    with incorruptibility,
and that which is mortal
    must clothe itself
    with immortality.

And when this which is
    corruptible clothes itself
    with incorruptibility
and this which is mortal
    clothes itself with
    immortality,
then the word that is written
    shall come about:
    Death is swallowed up in victory.
    Where, O death, is your victory?
    Where, O death, is your sting?

The sting of death is sin,
    and the power of sin is the law.
But thanks be to God who gives us
    the victory
    through our Lord Jesus Christ.

The word of the Lord.

Background of the Reading

St. Paul's writing is practical. We see that in this reading. Everyone will not die before Christ's return, yet all will be changed. Those who have died will rise to incorruptibility. Those still alive will become immortal. Paul concludes with a hymn that sings about victory over death. Its sting, or poison, is gone. Our loved one shares in that victory. They no longer need the law that can be difficult to keep. They and we share in resurrected freedom.

You might select this reading when the family of the loved one • • •
will draw comfort from hearing that we will be changed at the resurrection of the dead • will be consoled with knowing that Christ is victorious over death • needs to hear that those who die in Christ will be clothed with immortality.

If you select this reading, you might also consider • • •
Wisdom 4:7–15 **(FR–4)** • Revelation 14:13 **(FRE–2)** • Psalm 42:2, 3, 5cdef; 43:3, 4, 5 **(RP–4)** • Matthew 25:1–13 **(G–3)**

SR-9

What is seen is transitory, but what is unseen is eternal.

A reading from the second Letter of Saint Paul to the Corinthians

4:14—5:1

Brothers and sisters:
Knowing that the One who raised
the Lord Jesus
will raise us also with Jesus
and place us with you in
his presence.
Everything indeed is for you,
so that the grace bestowed
in abundance on more
and more people
may cause the thanksgiving
to overflow for the glory
of God.
Therefore, we are not discouraged;
rather, although our outer self
is wasting away,
our inner self is being renewed
day by day.

For this momentary light affliction
is producing for us an eternal
weight of glory beyond
all comparison,
as we look not to what is seen
but to what is unseen;
for what is seen is transitory,
but what is unseen is eternal.

For we know that if our earthly
dwelling, a tent,
should be destroyed,
we have a building from God,
a dwelling not made with hands,
eternal in heaven.

The word of the Lord.

Background of the Reading

St. Paul did not expect to live to see Christ's return at the end of time. He did expect to share in Christ's Resurrection. Our earthly bodies are like tents, temporary dwellings that last for a limited time. The glorious body that we will receive is a building from God, an eternal, sacred temple. These are words of hope. No matter the condition of our bodies at the time of death, they will be made glorious in the resurrection of our entire being, body and soul, made new and glorious with God.

You might select this reading when the family of the loved one . . .
seeks to hear that an eternal dwelling with God awaits us • is consoled by the proclamation that what is unseen matters more than what is seen • finds solace that the inner self is renewed as the outer wastes away.

If you select this reading, you might also consider . . .
Job 19:1, 23–27a **(FR–2)** • Revelation 21:1–5a, 6b–7 **(FRE–4)** • Psalm 122:1–2, 4–5, 6–7, 8–9 **(RP–8)** • John 11:32–45 **(G–15)**

SR–10

We have a building from God, eternal in heaven

A reading from the second Letter of Saint Paul to the Corinthians

5:1, 6–10

Brothers and sisters:
We know that if our earthly
    dwelling, a tent,
  should be destroyed,
  we have a building from God,
  a dwelling not made with hands,
  eternal in heaven.

We are always courageous,
  although we know that while
    we are at home in the body
  we are away from the Lord,
  for we walk by faith, not
    by sight.

Yet we are courageous,
  and we would rather leave
    the body and go home
    to the Lord.
Therefore, we aspire to please him,
  whether we are at home or away.
For we must all appear before the
    judgment seat of Christ,
  so that each may
    receive recompense,
  according to what he did in the
    body, whether good or evil.

The word of the Lord.

Background of the Reading

Paul's words reflect the fact that we love the bodily life that we know, and we seek to be with God forever. Ultimately, our desire for union with God is stronger than remaining in bodies ridden with pain and weakness. Then "we would rather leave the body and go home to the Lord." The way home is to walk by faith, please the Lord by doing his will, and come to stand with confidence before the judgment seat of Christ.

You might select this reading because your loved one • • •

was someone who looked toward dwelling in heaven • was an individual who understood the temporal nature of life • was a person of faith who wanted to please God.

If you select this reading, you might also consider • • •

Lamentations 3:17–26 **(FR–6)** • Revelation 14:13 **(FRE–2)** • Psalm 143:1–2, 5–6, 7ab and 8ab, 10 **(RP–10)** • Mark 15:33–39; 16:1–6 or 15:33–39 **(G–5)**

* * * * * * *

SR–11

He will change our lowly bodies to conform to his glory.

A reading from the Letter of Saint Paul to the Philippians
3:20–21

Brothers and sisters:
Our citizenship is in heaven,
  and from it we also await a savior, the Lord Jesus Christ.
He will change our lowly body
  to conform with his glorified Body
  by the power that enables him also
  to bring all things into subjection to himself.

The word of the Lord.

Background of the Reading

This brief, compact summary of the letter to the Philippians reiterates prominent Pauline themes: heavenly citizenship; the return of Christ, to whom all creation will be subject; and the change of the human body. These words offer hope to our deceased loved ones and to us. No matter what we suffer on earth, we will find freedom in heaven. Christ will return, take us there, and suffering will end. We will share in the glory of the Resurrection.

You might select this reading because your loved one • • •
was someone who knew that a Christian's true home is with God in heaven • was a faithful Christian who understood that all are subject to Christ, our king • was an individual who knew that Christ has power over all.

If you select this reading, you might also consider • • •
Isaiah 25:6a, 7–9 **(FR–5)** • Revelation 21:1–5a, 6b–7 **(FRE–4)** • Psalm 130:1–2, 3–4, 5–6ab, 6c–7, 8 **(RP–9)** • Luke 12:35–40 **(G–7)**

SR–12

Thus we shall always be with the Lord.

A reading from the first Letter of Saint Paul to the Thessalonians

4:13–18

We do not want you to be
unaware, brothers
and sisters,
about those who have
fallen asleep,
so that you may not grieve like
the rest, who have no hope.
For if we believe that Jesus died
and rose,
so too will God, through Jesus,
bring with him those who
have fallen asleep.
Indeed, we tell you this,
on the word of the Lord,
that we who are alive,
who are left until the coming
of the Lord,
will surely not precede those
who have fallen asleep.
For the Lord himself,
with a word of command,
with the voice of an archangel and
with the trumpet of God,
will come down from heaven,
and the dead in Christ will
rise first.
Then we who are alive, who are left,
will be caught up together with
them in the clouds
to meet the Lord in the air.
Thus we shall always be with
the Lord.
Therefore, console one another
with these words.

The word of the Lord.

Background of the Reading

Paul's utterly inclusive understanding of Christ's return is reflected in these consoling words. Those who have fallen asleep, who have died, will rise. Death is not the end. Then those who are living join them and "meet the Lord in the air." In Paul's worldview heaven was above and earth below, so Christ comes down to meet us and we go up to meet him. Belief in Jesus casts out fear and offers hope because "we shall always be with the Lord."

You might select this reading because your loved one . . .

was someone who knew that our hope is in Jesus Christ • was a person who trusted that all who have faith will be united in Christ • was a faithful Christian who looked forward to being reunited with friends and family in heaven.

If you select this reading, you might also consider . . .

Daniel 12:1–3 (**FR–7**) • Revelation 20:11—21:1 (**FRE–3**) • Psalm 27:1, 4, 7 and 8b and 9a, 13–14 (**RP–3**) • John 5:24–29 (**G–11**)

If we have died with him we shall also live with him.

A reading from the second Letter of Saint Paul to Timothy *2:8–13*

Beloved:
Remember Jesus Christ,
   raised from the dead,
   a descendant of David:
such is my Gospel, for which
   I am suffering,
even to the point of chains,
   like a criminal.
But the word of God is
   not chained.
Therefore, I bear with everything
   for the sake of those who
   are chosen,
so that they too may obtain
   the salvation that is in
   Christ Jesus,
together with eternal glory.
This saying is trustworthy:
   If we have died with him
     we shall also live with him;
   if we persevere
     we shall also reign with him.
But if we deny him
   he will deny us.
If we are unfaithful
   he remains faithful,
   for he cannot deny himself.

The word of the Lord.

Background of the Reading

Paul was imprisoned for preaching about Jesus Christ, and yet he continued to do so. God's Word cannot be chained. Suffering for the Gospel, he died with Christ. The last verses are a hymn. If we die with Christ, whether in Baptism or by living like Jesus, we will live with Christ. Those who faithfully live like Jesus will share in his glory. These words offer hope to someone who suffered for the Gospel. They remind mourners to be faithful to Christ, even in the face of difficulty.

You might select this reading because your loved one • • •
was a reader in the parish • was a participant in Scripture studies • was a faithful Christian who united their suffering to Christ.

If you select this reading, you might also consider • • •
Job 19:1, 23–27a **(FR–2)** • Acts 10:34–43 or 10:34–36, 42–43 **(FRE–1)** • Psalm 25:6 and 7b, 17–18, 20–21 **(RP–2)** • Matthew 5:1–12a **(G–1)**

SR–14

We shall see him as he is.

A reading from the first Letter of Saint John *3:1–2*

Beloved:
See what love the Father has bestowed on us
  that we may be called the children of God.
Yet so we are.
The reason the world does not know us
  is that it did not know him.
Beloved, we are God's children now;
  what we shall be has not yet been revealed.
We do know that when it is revealed we shall be like him,
  for we shall see him as he is.

The word of the Lord.

Background of the Reading

The letters of John share the same author as John's account of the Gospel, where love—God for us, us for God, and us for one another—is a dominant theme. It is God's love, made visible in Jesus, that makes us children of God, now. We know this because of our relationship with Jesus. If we continue to live the love that Christ shares with us, we will continue to be God's children so fully that we shall see God face to face. We can find comfort in this promise.

You might select this reading because your loved one · · ·
was a person who lived out the Christian life in prayer and service • was an individual regarded as holy • was someone who understood that mystery is part of faith.

If you select this reading, you might also consider · · ·
Wisdom 4:7–15 **(FR–4)** • Revelation 14:13 **(FRE–2)** • Psalm 23:1–3, 4, 5, 6 **(RP–1)** • Luke 7:11–17 **(G–6)**

SR–15

We know that we have passed from death to life because we love our brothers.

A reading from the first Letter of Saint John   *3:14–16*

Beloved:
We know that we have passed from death to life
  because we love our brothers.
Whoever does not love remains in death.
Everyone who hates his brother is a murderer,
  and you know that no murderer has eternal life remaining in him.
The way we came to know love
  was that he laid down his life for us;
  so we ought to lay down our lives for our brothers.

The word of the Lord.

Background of the Reading

The letter of John is clear: concrete love is what enables us to pass from death to life. We must show our belonging to Jesus by imitating his unconditional, sacrificial love on the Cross. In other words, do unto others what Christ has done for us. If our deeds show that we did this, we can meet earthly death and pass over into eternal life. This is true for our deceased loved one and serves to remind us how to live until our own time comes to pass from death to life.

You might select this reading because your loved one ● ● ●

was someone who stayed reconciled with others • was an individual who did not let past wrongs hinder relationship • was a person who was willing to forgive.

If you select this reading, you might also consider ● ● ●

Wisdom 3:1–9 or 3:1–6, 9 **(FR–3)** • Revelation 14:13 **(FRE–2)** • Psalm 116:5, 6, 10–11, 15–16ac **(RP–7)** • John 6:37–40 **(G–12)**

The Alleluia Verse and Verse before the Gospel (Gospel Acclamation)

Following the Second Reading, there is a period of silence. Then all stand for the Acclamation before the Gospel. This acclamation is usually "Alleluia" (except during Lent) and is always sung by the assembly. A verse from Scripture, sung by a cantor or choir, follows the Acclamation, after which all repeat the sung refrain. In this section, you will find eleven options from which to select as the verse (**GA–1** to **GA–11**). Your parish staff will be able to help you select an appropriate musical setting.

GA–1
Blessed are you, Father, Lord of heaven and earth;
you have revealed to the childlike the mysteries of the Kingdom.
—See Matthew 11:25

GA–2
Come, you who are blessed by my Father, says the Lord;
inherit the kingdom prepared for you from the foundation
of the world.
—Matthew 25:34

GA–3
God so loved the world that he gave his only-begotten Son,
so that everyone who believes in him might have eternal life.
—John 3:16

GA–4

This is the will of my Father, says the Lord,
that I should lose nothing of all that he has given to me,
and that I should raise it up on the last day
—John 6:39

GA–5

This is the will of my Father, says the Lord,
that everyone who sees the Son and believes in him
may have eternal life,
and I shall raise him on the last day.
—John 6:40

GA–6

I am the living bread that came down from heaven,
says the Lord;
whoever eats this bread will live forever.
—John 6:51a

GA–7

I am the resurrection and the life, says the Lord;
whoever believes in me will never die.
—John 11:25a, 26

GA–8

Our true home is in heaven,
and Jesus Christ, whose return we long for,
will come from heaven to save us.
—See Philippians 3:20

GA–9

If we die with Christ, we shall live with him,
and if we persevere we shall also reign with him.
—2 Timothy 2:11-12a

GA–10

Jesus Christ is the firstborn from the dead;
glory and power be his forever and ever. Amen.
—Revelation 1:5a, 6b

GA–11

Blessed are those who have died in the Lord;
let them rest from their labors for their good deeds go with them.
—Revelation 14:13

The Gospel

The Gospel at a Catholic funeral comes from one of the four New Testament Gospel accounts: Matthew, Mark, Luke, and John. *Gospel* means "Good News." There are nineteen passages from which to choose, found in this chapter numbered **G-1**, **G-2**, and so on. As you read these passages, you will hear Good News about Jesus being one with God, that he is the living bread who quenches our hunger and thirst, and how he too faced death in others and himself.

Connect the Good News of Jesus Christ with the good news of your loved one's life. Hear how Christ seeks to comfort you and those who celebrate this funeral. Feed on Christ's words of life. Find hope and strength in them to witness your faith in the Resurrection.

If you are not sure what reading to choose, your pastor or whomever you are meeting with to prepare the funeral can help.

• • • • •

G–1

Rejoice and be glad for your reward will be great in heaven.

A reading from the holy Gospel according to Matthew   *5:1–12a*

When Jesus saw the crowds,
    he went up the mountain,
and after he had sat down,
    his disciples came to him.
He began to teach them, saying:
    "Blessed are the poor in spirit,
        for theirs is the Kingdom
        of heaven.
Blessed are they who mourn,
    for they will be comforted.
Blessed are the meek,
    for they will inherit the land.
Blessed are they who hunger and
    thirst for righteousness,
    for they will be satisfied.
Blessed are the merciful,
    for they will be shown mercy.

Blessed are the clean of heart,
    for they will see God.
Blessed are the peacemakers,
    for they will be called
        children of God.
Blessed are they who are
    persecuted for the sake
    of righteousness,
    for theirs is the Kingdom
    of heaven.
Blessed are you when they insult
    you and persecute you
    and utter every kind of evil
        against you falsely
        because of me.
Rejoice and be glad,
    for your reward will be great
    in heaven."

The Gospel of the Lord.

Background of the Reading

In this reading Jesus has the posture of a teacher, whose students are gathered to learn the *attitudes* needed to *be* his disciples. They are: dependence upon God, compassion, humility, right relationship with God, mercy, desire for God alone, peacemaking, and fidelity in the face of opposition. Those who lived these attitudes will receive God's compassion and inherit the kingdom of heaven. We will also be blessed if we learn and live these beatitudes.

You might select this reading because your loved one • • •
sought to live out God's mercy and forgiveness by acting on behalf of others •
served as a peacemaker • possessed a pure heart.

If you select this reading, you might also consider • • •
Job 19:1, 23–27a **(FR–2)** • Acts 10:34–43 or 10:34–36, 42–43 **(FRE–1)** •
Psalm 25:6 and 7b, 17–18, 20–21 **(RP–2)** • 2 Timothy 2:8–13 **(SR–13)**

• • • • •

G–2
Come to me and I will give you rest.

A reading from the holy Gospel according to Matthew *11:25–30*

At that time Jesus answered:
"I give praise to you, Father, Lord of heaven and earth,
   for although you have hidden these things
   from the wise and the learned
   you have revealed them to the childlike.
Yes, Father, such has been your gracious will.
All things have been handed over to me by my Father.
No one knows the Son except the Father,
   and no one knows the Father except the Son
   and anyone to whom the Son wishes to reveal him.

"Come to me, all you who labor and are burdened,
   and I will give you rest.
Take my yoke upon you and learn from me,
   for I am meek and humble of heart;
   and you will find rest for yourselves.
For my yoke is easy, and my burden light."

The Gospel of the Lord.

Background of the Reading

Jesus prays aloud to the Father, with whom Jesus shared a unique and intimate relationship. For Matthew's Jewish audience, his words make clear that Jesus reveals the Father in ways that are less burdensome than the Law. By taking on Jesus' yoke, by seeking and living the will of God, we find rest. These are words of assurance for someone who followed God's will, and hope to mourners, who still have time to bear the light burden of Jesus' yoke.

You might select this reading because your loved one • • •
had a childlike faith in God • worked hard in physical labor •
suffered many hardships throughout life.

If you select this reading, you might also consider • • •
Isaiah 25:6a, 7–9 **(FR–5)** • Revelation 14:13 **(FRE–2)** • Psalm 103:8 and 10,
13–14, 15–16, 17–18 **(RP–6)** • Romans 5:17–21 **(SR–2)**

• • • • •

G–3

Behold the bridegroom! Come out to him!

A reading from the holy Gospel according to Matthew   *25:1–13*

Jesus told his disciples this parable:
"The Kingdom of heaven will be like ten virgins
  who took their lamps and went out to meet the bridegroom.
Five of them were foolish and five were wise.
The foolish ones, when taking their lamps,
  brought no oil with them,
  but the wise brought flasks of oil with their lamps.
Since the bridegroom was long delayed,
  they all became drowsy and fell asleep.
At midnight, there was a cry,
  'Behold, the bridegroom! Come out to meet him!'
Then all those virgins got up and trimmed their lamps.
The foolish ones said to the wise,
  'Give us some of your oil,
  for our lamps are going out.'
But the wise ones replied,
  'No, for there may not be enough for us and you.
Go instead to the merchants and buy some for yourselves.'
While they went off to buy it,
  the bridegroom came
  and those who were ready went into the wedding feast with him.
Then the door was locked.
Afterwards the other virgins came and said,
  'Lord, Lord, open the door for us!'
But he said in reply,
  'Amen, I say to you, I do not know you.'
Therefore, stay awake,
  for you know neither the day nor the hour."

The Gospel of the Lord.

Background of the Reading

This parable calls us to be ready whenever our life ends by keeping the light of Christ received at Baptism burning, like the wise virgins kept their lamps burning. The foolish virgins thought they had time, but they were wrong. We must ready ourselves, no matter who offers to help us. We are both wise and foolish at times. Since we know neither the day nor the hour, seek to be ready at all times. Then we will enter the feast of heaven whenever our time comes.

You might select this reading because your loved one • • •

stayed alert to the ways of the Lord • prepared for death by keeping a close relationship with God • always attended to his or her spiritual life.

If you select this reading, you might also consider • • •

Wisdom 4:7–15 (**FR–4**) • Revelation 14:13 (**FRE–2**) • Psalm 42:2, 3, 5cdef; 43:3, 4, 5 (**RP–4**) • 1 Corinthians 15:51–57 (**SR–8**)

• • • • •

G–4

Come, you who are blessed by my Father.

A reading from the holy Gospel according to Matthew   *25:31–46*

Jesus said to his disciples:
"When the Son of Man comes in his glory,
  and all the angels with him,
  he will sit upon his glorious throne,
  and all the nations will be assembled before him.
And he will separate them one from another,
  as a shepherd separates the sheep from the goats.
He will place the sheep on his right and the goats on his left.
Then the king will say to those on his right,
  'Come, you who are blessed by my Father.
Inherit the kingdom prepared for you from the foundation of the world.
For I was hungry and you gave me food,
  I was thirsty and you gave me drink,
  a stranger and you welcomed me,
  naked and you clothed me,
  ill and you cared for me,
  in prison and you visited me.'
Then the righteous will answer him and say,
  'Lord, when did we see you hungry and feed you,
  or thirsty and give you drink?
When did we see you a stranger and welcome you,
  or naked and clothe you?
When did we see you ill or in prison, and visit you?'
And the king will say to them in reply,
  'Amen, I say to you, whatever you did
  for one of these least brothers of mine, you did for me.'
Then he will say to those on his left,
  'Depart from me, you accursed,
  into the eternal fire prepared for the Devil and his angels.

For I was hungry and you gave me no food,
  I was thirsty and you gave me no drink,
  a stranger and you gave me no welcome,
  naked and you gave me no clothing,
  ill and in prison, and you did not care for me.'
Then they will answer and say,
  'Lord, when did we see you hungry or thirsty
  or a stranger or naked or ill or in prison,
  and not minister to your needs?'
He will answer them, 'Amen, I say to you,
  what you did not do for one of these least ones,
  you did not do for me.'
And these will go off to eternal punishment,
  but the righteous to eternal life."

The Gospel of the Lord.

Background of the Reading

Here we have Matthew's "Final Exam" in his school for following Jesus. Others see Jesus by living the corporal (bodily) works of mercy: feeding the hungry, clothing the naked, giving drink to the thirsty, visiting the imprisoned, caring for the sick, welcoming the stranger, and caring for creation. These works make clear whether or not someone was one of Jesus' followers. This Gospel affirms the faith of someone known for living these works and invites family and friends to follow their example.

You might select this reading because your loved one • • •
helped out in a soup kitchen • ministered to those who were hungry, thirsty, or homeless, or cared for creation • volunteered in prison ministry.

If you select this reading, you might also consider • • •
Lamentations 3:17–26 **(FR–6)** • Revelation 20:11—21:1 **(FRE–3)** • Psalm 27:1, 4, 7 and 8b and 9a, 13–14 **(RP–3)** • Romans 14:7–9, 10c–12 **(SR–6)**

G–5

Jesus gave a loud cry and breathed his last.

A reading from the holy Gospel according to Mark

Long form: 15:33–39; 16:1–6 [*Short form: 15:33–39*]

[At noon darkness came over the whole land
  until three in the afternoon.
And at three o'clock Jesus cried out in a loud voice,
  "Eloi, Eloi, lema sabachthani?"
  which is translated,
  "My God, my God, why have you forsaken me?"
Some of the bystanders who heard it said,
  "Look, he is calling Elijah."
One of them ran, soaked a sponge with wine, put it on a reed,
  and gave it to him to drink, saying,
  "Wait, let us see if Elijah comes to take him down."
Jesus gave a loud cry and breathed his last.
The veil of the sanctuary was torn in two from top to bottom.
When the centurion who stood facing him
  saw how he breathed his last he said,
  "Truly this man was the Son of God!"]

When the sabbath was over,
  Mary Magdalene, Mary, the mother of James, and Salome
  bought spices so that they might go and anoint him.
Very early when the sun had risen,
  on the first day of the week, they came to the tomb.
They were saying to one another,
  "Who will roll back the stone for us
  from the entrance to the tomb?"
When they looked up,
  they saw that the stone had been rolled back;
  it was very large.
On entering the tomb they saw a young man
  sitting on the right side, clothed in a white robe,
  and they were utterly amazed.

He said to them, "Do not be amazed!
You seek Jesus of Nazareth, the crucified.
He has been raised; he is not here.
Behold the place where they laid him."

The Gospel of the Lord.

Background of the Reading

In the Gospel according to Mark, Jesus, the Son of God, is very human. He quotes familiar words from Psalm 22 as a cry of trust in God's vindication of his life. He cries out in pain at the point of death. Concrete and concise, it is a nonbeliever who calls Jesus, Son of God. His own did not. The faithful women find an empty tomb, meet an angel, and hear that Jesus is raised. These simple and direct words offer hope for one who simply sought the Lord and trusted God, even in suffering.

You might select this reading when the family of the loved one ● ● ●
will draw comfort from hearing that death has no power ● will be consoled by the promise of eternal life ● needs the assurance that Christ was raised from the dead and redeemed us from our sins.

If you select this reading, you might also consider ● ● ●
Job 19:1, 23–27a **(FR–2)** ● Revelation 21:1–5a, 6b–7 **(FRE–4)** ● Psalm 122:1–2, 4–5, 6–7, 8–9 **(RP–8)** ● 2 Corinthians 5:1, 6–10 **(SR–10)**

• • • • •

G–6

Young man, I tell you, arise!

A reading from the holy Gospel according to Luke   *7:11–17*

Jesus journeyed to a city
     called Nain,
   and his disciples and a large
     crowd accompanied him.
As he drew near to the gate
     of the city,
   a man who had died was
     being carried out,
   the only son of his mother,
     and she was a widow.
A large crowd from the city
     was with her.
When the Lord saw her,
   he was moved with pity
     for her and said to her,
   "Do not weep."
He stepped forward and
     touched the coffin;
   at this the bearers halted,
   and he said, "Young man,
     I tell you, arise!"
The dead man sat up and began
     to speak,
   and Jesus gave him to his mother.
Fear seized them all, and they
     glorified God, exclaiming,
   "A great prophet has arisen
     in our midst,"
   and "God has visited his people."
This report about him spread
     through the whole of Judea
   and in all the surrounding region.

The Gospel of the Lord.

Background of the Reading

This reading manifests the compassion of Jesus and his care for women, two themes in Luke's account of the Gospel. Here we hear the word, *Lord*, for the first time in Luke. It identifies Jesus with the all-powerful God of Israel. Raising the widow's son affirms Jesus' power. The people give God glory for visiting them in Jesus. These are words of compassion, faith that God can bring life out of death, and are a vehicle for God to visit the family and friends of your loved one.

You might select this reading when the family of the loved one • • •
will be consoled hearing that Christ has power over death • will be comforted that Christ weeps with those who mourn • needs the assurance that eternal life awaits when we die.

If you select this reading, you might also consider • • •
Wisdom 4:7–15 **(FR–4)** • Revelation 14:13 **(FRE–2)** • Psalm 23:1–3, 4, 5, 6 **(RP–1)** • 1 John 3:1–2 **(SR–14)**

G–7

You also must be prepared.

A reading from the holy Gospel according to Luke   *12:35–40*

Jesus said to his disciples:
"Gird your loins and light your lamps
   and be like servants who await their master's return from a wedding,
   ready to open immediately when he comes and knocks.
Blessed are those servants
   whom the master finds vigilant on his arrival.
Amen, I say to you, he will gird himself,
   have them recline at table, and proceed to wait on them.
And should he come in the second or third watch
   and find them prepared in this way,
   blessed are those servants.
Be sure of this:
   if the master of the house had known the hour
   when the thief was coming,
   he would not have let his house be broken into.
You also must be prepared, for at an hour you do not expect,
   the Son of Man will come."

The Gospel of the Lord.

Background of the Reading

Like Matthew 25:1–13 (**G–3**), Luke tells us to be ready for Jesus' return at all times. Loins that are girt symbolize readiness. One's robe is tucked into one's belt, to be ready to move. Lit lamps symbolize the light needed to welcome and follow Jesus, who serves us at the heavenly wedding feast. Jesus is on a journey to Jerusalem in this part of Luke's account of the Gospel. Life is a journey to the heavenly Jerusalem. With eyes fixed on Jesus, we are always ready.

You might select this reading because your loved one ● ● ●
cared for the needs of the soul • was vigilant in his or her relationship with God • tended to be prepared for any crises.

If you select this reading, you might also consider ● ● ●
Isaiah 25:6a, 7–9 (**FR–5**) • Revelation 21:1–5a, 6b–7 (**FRE–4**) • Psalm 130:1–2, 3–4, 5–6ab, 6c–7, 8 (**RP–9**) • Philippians 3:20–21 (**SR–11**)

G–8

Today you will be with me in paradise.

A reading from the holy Gospel according to Luke   *23:33, 39–43*

When the soldiers came to the
place called the Skull,
they crucified Jesus and the
criminals there,
one on his right,
the other on his left.

Now one of the criminals
hanging there
reviled Jesus, saying,
"Are you not the Christ?
Save yourself and us."
The other man, however,
rebuking him, said in reply,
"Have you no fear of God,
for you are subject to the same
condemnation?

And indeed, we have been
condemned justly,
for the sentence we
received corresponds
toour crimes,
but this man has done
nothing criminal."
Then he said,
"Jesus, remember me when
you come into your
Kingdom."
He replied to him,
"Amen, I say to you,
today you will be with me
in Paradise."

The word of the Lord.

Background of the Reading

The evangelist, Luke, refers to the place of Jesus' Crucifixion as "the Skull." In death as in life, Jesus loves all. His response to the justly condemned criminal affirms that God's mercy is for you: "today you will be with me in Paradise." For the Gospel writer, Luke, Paradise is not a place. It names the condition of following Jesus in one's heart. Today, "now," you will share my glory. So can our deceased loved one. So can we.

You might select this reading because your loved one • • •

looked to the Lord for forgiveness • would come to another's aid • approached God and others humbly.

If you select this reading, you might also consider • • •

Wisdom 3:1–9 or 3:1–6, 9 **(FR–3)** • Revelation 21:1–5a, 6b–7 **(FRE–4)** • Psalm 116:5, 6, 10–11, 15–16ac **(RP–7)** • Romans 5:5–11 **(SR–1)**

G–9

Father, into your hands I commend my spirit.

A reading from the holy Gospel according to Luke

Long form: 23:44–46, 50, 52–53; 24:1–6a [Short form: 23:44–46, 50–53]

[It was about noon and darkness came over the whole land
   until three in the afternoon
   because of an eclipse of the sun.
Then the veil of the temple was torn down the middle.
Jesus cried out in a loud voice,
   "Father, into your hands I commend my spirit";
   and when he had said this he breathed his last.

Now there was a virtuous and righteous man
named Joseph who,
   though he was a member of the council,
   went to Pilate and asked for the Body of Jesus.
After he had taken the Body down,
   he wrapped it in a linen cloth
   and laid him in a rock-hewn tomb
   in which no one had yet been buried.]

At daybreak on the first day of the week
   the women took the spices they had prepared
   and went to the tomb.
They found the stone rolled away from the tomb;
   but when they entered,
   they did not find the Body of the Lord Jesus.
While they were puzzling over this, behold,
   two men in dazzling garments appeared to them.
They were terrified and bowed their faces to the ground.
They said to them,
   "Why do you seek the living one among the dead?
He is not here, but he has been raised."

The Gospel of the Lord.

Background of the Reading

Luke is concise in telling these events. Jesus, fully conscious, quotes Psalm 31:6 and submits his life to God. The torn Temple veil means all can share God's merciful love. Followers, like Joseph and the women, honored Jesus' body as faith required. The two men in dazzling garments recall the Transfiguration, and Jesus' revealed glory is offered to us. Look for him among the living. Celebrate what our faith requires, and share in Christ's glorious Resurrection.

You might select this reading because your loved one . . .

acted virtuously and looked after the needs of the community • lived righteously and would speak up for others • led a moral life and ministered to the marginalized.

If you select this reading, you might also consider . . .

Daniel 12:1–3 **(FR–7)** • Acts 10:34–43 or 10:34–36, 42–43 **(FRE–1)** • Psalm 23:1–3, 4, 5, 6 **(RP–1)** • Romans 8:31b–35, 37–39 **(SR–5)**

G–10

Was it not necessary that the Christ should suffer these things and enter into his glory?

A reading from the holy Gospel according to Luke

Long form: 24:13-35 [*Short form: 24:13-16, 28-35*]

[That very day, the first day of the week,
  two of the disciples of Jesus were going
  to a village called Emmaus, seven miles from Jerusalem,
  and they were conversing about all the things that had occurred.
And it happened that while they were conversing and debating,
  Jesus himself drew near and walked with them,
  but their eyes were prevented from recognizing him.]
He asked them,
  "What are you discussing as you walk along?"
They stopped, looking downcast.
One of them, named Cleopas, said to him in reply,
  "Are you the only visitor to Jerusalem
  who does not know of the things
  that have taken place there in these days?"
And he replied to them, "What sort of things?"
They said to him,
  "The things that happened to Jesus the Nazarene,
  who was a prophet mighty in deed and word
  before God and all the people,
  how our chief priests and rulers both handed him over
  to a sentence of death and crucified him.
But we were hoping that he would be the one to redeem Israel;
  and besides all this,
  it is now the third day since this took place.
Some women from our group, however, have astounded us:
  they were at the tomb early in the morning
  and did not find his Body;
  they came back and reported
  that they had indeed seen a vision of angels
  who announced that he was alive.

Then some of those with us went to the tomb
and found things just as the women had described,
but him they did not see."
And he said to them, "Oh, how foolish you are!
How slow of heart to believe all that the prophets spoke!
Was it not necessary that the Christ should suffer these things
and enter into his glory?"
Then beginning with Moses and all the prophets,
Jesus interpreted to them what referred to him
in all the Scriptures.
[As they approached the village to which they were going,
Jesus gave the impression that he was going on farther.
But they urged him, "Stay with us,
for it is nearly evening and the day is almost over."
So he went in to stay with them.
And it happened that, while he was with them at table,
he took bread, said the blessing,
broke it, and gave it to them.
With that their eyes were opened and they recognized him,
but he vanished from their sight.
Then they said to each other,
"Were not our hearts burning within us
while he spoke to us on the way and opened the Scriptures to us?"
So they set out at once and returned to Jerusalem
where they found gathered together
the Eleven and those with them, who were saying,
"The Lord has truly been raised and has appeared to Simon!"
Then the two recounted
what had taken place on the way
and how he was made known to them in the breaking of the bread.]

The Gospel of the Lord.

Background of the Reading

On "that very day," the Lucan "now" of faith, the disciples meet Jesus, but don't know it yet. Their darkness becomes light as Jesus walks with them, hears their story, and illuminates the Scriptures for them. They invite him to stay, and the four-fold actions of the Eucharist— take, bless, break, and eat—opens their eyes. Recognizing him, they go to share their "heart burn," their belief in him as resurrected Lord. Gathering for the funeral Mass can do the same for us.

You might select this reading because your loved one ● ● ●

possessed a heart that burned with desire to know the Lord more deeply ● encountered Christ in Scripture and the Eucharist ● understood Christ as living in our midst.

If you select this reading, you might also consider ● ● ●

Wisdom 3:1–9 or 3:1–6, 9 **(FR–3)** ● Acts 10:34–43 or 10:34–36, 42–43 **(FRE–1)** ● Psalm 63:2, 3–4, 5–6, 6–9 **(RP–5)** ● Romans 8:14–23 **(SR–4)**

G–11

Whoever hears my word and believes has passed from death to life.

A reading from the holy Gospel according to John   *5:24-29*

Jesus answered the Jews
 and said to them:
"Amen, amen, I say to you,
 whoever hears my word
and believes in the one
 who sent me
has eternal life and will not
 come to condemnation,
but has passed from death to life.
Amen, amen, I say to you, the hour
 is coming and is now here
when the dead will hear the voice
 of the Son of God,
and those who hear will live.

For just as the Father has life
 in himself,
 so also he gave to the Son the
 possession of life in himself.
And he gave him power
 to exercise judgment,
because he is the Son of Man.
Do not be amazed at this,
because the hour is coming in
 which all who are in the tombs
will hear his voice and
 will come out,
those who have done good deeds
 to the resurrection of life,
but those who have done
 wicked deeds
to the resurrection of
 condemnation."

The Gospel of the Lord.

Background of the Reading

In John's account of the Gospel, Jesus shares eternal life with those who hear his Word and believe in the Father. The fullness of that life is also a future promise. When Jesus returns, those who have done good will rise to glory with Jesus. Those who did evil will share eternal condemnation. Jesus' redeeming love is a present reality and a future promise. We have a choice, do good or evil. How we live here makes known the kind of eternity we will share. These words comfort and invite.

You might select this reading because your loved one • • •
had a love for Scripture • performed good deeds • listened for God's voice.

If you select this reading, you might also consider • • •
Daniel 12:1–3 (**FR–7**) • Revelation 14:13 (**FRE–2**) • Psalm 27:1, 4, 7 and 8b and 9a, 13–14 (**RP–3**) • Thessalonians 4:13–18 (**SR–12**)

G–12

Everyone who sees the Son and believes in him may have eternal life and I shall raise him on the last day.

A reading from the holy Gospel according to John   *6:37–40*

Jesus said to the crowds:
"Everything that the Father gives me will come to me,
  and I will not reject anyone who comes to me,
  because I came down from heaven not to do my own will
  but the will of the one who sent me.
And this is the will of the one who sent me,
  that I should not lose anything of what he gave me,
  but that I should raise it on the last day.
For this is the will of my Father,
  that everyone who sees the Son and believes in him
  may have eternal life,
  and I shall raise him on the last day."

The Gospel of the Lord.

Background of the Reading

These words are part of the Bread of Life discourse from the Gospel according to John. Jesus lives God's will. God promises that everyone who sees and believes in Jesus can share resurrected life. That's the bread that Jesus feeds us, a share in life everlasting, so those who have a relationship with Jesus need not fear death. These are words of hope to believers. They encourage us to develop a relationship with him, for God desires not to lose anything God gave Jesus, including us.

You might select this reading because your loved one • • •
sought God in prayer • felt that he or she belonged to God • tried to stay close to God.

If you select this reading, you might also consider • • •
Wisdom 3:1–9 or 3:1–6, 9 **(FR–3)** • Revelation 21:1–5a, 6b–7 **(FRE–4)** • Psalm 116:5, 6, 10–11, 15–16ac **(RP–7)** • 1 John 3:14–16 **(SR–15)**

Whoever eats this bread will live forever, and I will raise them on the last day.

A reading from the holy Gospel according to John   *6:51–59*

Jesus said to the crowds:
"I am the living bread that came down from heaven;
   whoever eats this bread will live forever;
   and the bread that I will give is my Flesh
   for the life of the world."

The Jews quarreled among themselves, saying,
   "How can this man give us his Flesh to eat?"
Jesus said to them,
   "Amen, amen, I say to you,
   unless you eat the Flesh of the Son of Man and drink his Blood,
   you do not have life within you.
Whoever eats my Flesh and drinks my Blood
   has eternal life,
   and I will raise him on the last day.
For my Flesh is true food,
   and my Blood is true drink.
Whoever eats my Flesh and drinks my Blood
   remains in me and I in him.
Just as the living Father sent me
   and I have life because of the Father,
   so also the one who feeds on me
   will have life because of me.
This is the bread that came down from heaven.
Unlike your ancestors who ate and still died,
   whoever eats this bread will live forever."

The Gospel of the Lord.

Background of the Reading

These words continue John's teaching about Jesus as the Bread of Life. Just as God became one with humanity in Jesus, God-made-flesh, we become one with God by our communion with Christ in the Eucharist. Jesus is talking about more than mere food and drink, which his hearers could not see. In him we share the very life of God, a life that continues beyond physical death. We share that life in the funeral Mass, like our loved one, who celebrated the Eucharist on a regular basis.

You might select this reading because your loved one ...

found spiritual nourishment in the Eucharist • believed the Real Presence of Christ in the Eucharist offered new life • understood the Eucharist as the way God nourishes the world.

If you select this reading, you might also consider ...

Isaiah 25:6a, 7–9 **(FR–5)** • Acts 10:34–43 or 10:34–36, 42–43 **(FRE–1)** • Psalm 23:1–3, 4, 5, 6 **(RP–1)** • Romans 6:3–9 or 6:3–4, 8–9 **(SR–3)**

I am the resurrection and the life.

A reading from the holy Gospel accoridng to John

Long form: 11:17–27 [*Short form: 11:21–27*]

When Jesus arrived in Bethany, he found that Lazarus
  had already been in the tomb for four days.
Now Bethany was near Jerusalem, only about two miles away.
Many of the Jews had come to Martha and Mary
  to comfort them about their brother.
When Martha heard that Jesus was coming,
  she went to meet him;
  but Mary sat at home.
[Martha said to Jesus,
  "Lord, if you had been here,
  my brother would not have died.
But even now I know that whatever you ask of God,
  God will give you."
Jesus said to her,
  "Your brother will rise."
Martha said to him,
  "I know he will rise,
  in the resurrection on the last day."
Jesus told her,
  "I am the resurrection and the life;
  whoever believes in me, even if he dies, will live,
  and everyone who lives and believes in me will never die.
Do you believe this?"
He said to him, "Yes, Lord.
I have come to believe that you are the Christ, the Son of God,
  the one who is coming into the world."]

The Gospel of the Lord.

Background of the Reading

Some of the Jews at this time believed that the spirit left the body after being dead for three days. Jesus arrives after that time. Martha, Lazarus' sister, also reflects a belief of some Jews in the resurrection on the last day. Jesus identifies himself as "the resurrection and the life." To believe in him is to share in his Resurrection. If, like Martha, we profess faith in Jesus as God's anointed, the Christ, we will also rise. We gather to express that faith.

You might select this reading when the family of the loved one • • •
will be comforted by knowing that God will always listen to them • draws consolation from hearing that those who believe will have eternal life • will find comfort that death does not have the last word.

If you select this reading, you might also consider • • •
Wisdom 4:7–15 **(FR–4)** • Revelation 14:13 **(FRE–2)** • Psalm 42:2, 3, 5cdef; 43:3, 4, 5 **(RP–4)** • 1 Corinthians 15:51–57 **(SR–8)**

. . . . . .

G–15

Lazarus, come out!

A reading from the holy Gospel according to John   *11:32–45*

When Mary came to where Jesus was and saw him,
    she fell at his feet and said to him,
    "Lord, if you had been here,
    my brother would not have died."
When Jesus saw her weeping and the Jews who had come with
        her weeping,
    he became perturbed and deeply troubled, and said,
    "Where have you laid him?"
They said to him, "Sir, come and see."
And Jesus wept.
So the Jews said, "See how he loved him."
But some of them said,
    "Could not the one who opened the eyes of the blind man
    have done something so that this man would not have died?"

So Jesus, perturbed again, came to the tomb.
It was a cave, and a stone lay across it.
Jesus said, "Take away the stone."
Martha, the dead man's sister, said to him,
    "Lord, by now there will be a stench;
    he has been dead for four days."
Jesus said to her,
    "Did I not tell you that if you believe
    you will see the glory of God?"
So they took away the stone.
And Jesus raised his eyes and said,
    "Father, I thank you for hearing me.
I know that you always hear me;
    but because of the crowd here I have said this,
    that they may believe that you sent me."
And when he had said this,
    he cried out in a loud voice,
    "Lazarus, come out!"

The dead man came out,
  tied hand and foot with burial bands,
  and his face was wrapped in a cloth.
So Jesus said to the crowd,
  "Untie him and let him go."

Now many of Jews who had come to Mary
  and seen what he had done began to believe in him.

The Gospel of the Lord.

Background of the Reading

Typical of John, a human encounter reveals Jesus' divinity. Jesus weeps. His friend died and people are grieving, which expresses their frustration that God did not heal Lazarus. Jesus goes to the tomb and its stench. He faces death and prays aloud as a sign of his unique relationship with God. He'd said that the dead would hear his voice and rise. Lazarus does. The crowd frees Lazarus. We gather in our grief to find God and ask for new life, for our loved one and for us.

You might select this reading when the family of the loved one . . .
needs to know that God listens to us when we are distressed • will be comforted by God's power over death • will be strengthened from hearing that God's glory awaits the dead.

If you select this reading, you might also consider . . .
Job 19:1, 23–27a **(FR–2)** • Revelation 21:1–5a, 6b–7 **(FRE–4)** • Psalm 122:1–2, 4–5, 6–7, 8–9 **(RP–8)** • 2 Corinthians 4:14—5:1 **(SR–9)**

If it dies, it produces much fruit.

A reading from the holy Gospel according to John

Long form: 12:23–28 [Short form: 12:23–26]

[Jesus said to his disciples:
"The hour has come for the Son
    of Man to be glorified.
Amen, amen, I say to you,
  unless a grain of wheat falls
    to the ground and dies,
  it remains just a grain of wheat;
  but if it dies, it produces
    much fruit.
Whoever loves his life will lose it,
  and whoever hates his life
    in this world
  will preserve it for eternal life.

Whoever serves me must follow me,
  and where I am, there also will
    my servant be.
The Father will honor whoever
    serves me.]

"I am troubled now. Yet what
    should I say?
'Father, save me from this hour'?
But it was for this purpose
    that I came to this hour.
Father, glorify your name."
Then a voice came from heaven,
  "I have glorified it and will
    glorify it again."

The Gospel of the Lord.

Background of the Reading

John points out that life is filled with paradox: only by dying or being transformed does the grain of wheat bear fruit; only by serving others or dying to being self-centered do human beings live. Dying and rising are intimately connected. The same is true of faith. By dying to self and living for or serving others, like Jesus, we find fullness of life. We often wish that we could live here forever. We can't. But, like Jesus, when our lives give God glory, so do our deaths, and we live.

You might select this reading when the family of the loved one • • •
will be comforted with the knowledge that our lives are preserved for eternal life • needs to hear that those who followed the Lord will be with him in the next life • will be consoled that those who honor God are honored for eternity.

If you select this reading, you might also consider • • •
Isaiah 25:6a, 7–9 **(FR–5)** • Revelation 20:11—21:1 **(FRE–3)** • Psalm 23:1–3, 4, 5, 6 **(RP–1)** • 1 Corinthians 15:20–28 or 15:20–23 **(SR–7)**

G–17

In my father's house there are many dwellings.

A reading from the holy Gospel according to John   *14:1–6*

Jesus said to his disciples:
"Do not let your hearts be troubled.
You have faith in God; have faith also in me.
In my Father's house there are many dwelling places.
If there were not,
 would I have told you that I am going to prepare a place for you?
And if I go and prepare a place for you,
 I will come back again and take you to myself,
 so that where I am you also may be.
Where I am going you know the way."
Thomas said to him,
 "Master, we do not know where you are going;
 how can we know the way?"
Jesus said to him, "I am the way and the truth and the life.
No one comes to the Father except through me."

The Gospel of the Lord.

Background of the Reading

In the Bible, this passage follows Jesus' announcement that he is going to the Father. He reassures his disciples, who are afraid, that he is not abandoning them. No, God is here, for his dwelling places are both in heaven and wherever Jesus' followers are. Jesus is "I am," the name God revealed to Moses. He shows us the way to God. He shares with us the truth of God's way. He gives us eternal life. We gather to find reassurance in the promise that God is with our loved one and with us.

You might select this reading because your loved one ● ● ●
was comforted by knowing that a dwelling in heaven was suited to each person ● was someone who searched for the truth ● needed reassurance that God was awaiting him or her.

If you select this reading, you might also consider ● ● ●
Isaiah 25:6a, 7–9 **(FR–5)** ● Revelation 21:1–5a, 6b–7 **(FRE–4)** ● Psalm 27:1, 4, 7 and 8b and 9a, 13–14 **(RP–3)** ● 1 John 3:1–2 **(SR–14)**

G–18

I wish that where I am they also may be with me.

A reading from the holy Gospel according to John   *17:24–26*

Jesus raised his eyes to heaven and said:
"Father, those whom you gave me are your gift to me.
I wish that where I am they also may be with me,
  that they may see my glory that you gave me,
  because you loved me before the foundation of the world.
Righteous Father, the world also does not know you,
  but I know you, and they know that you sent me.
I made known to them your name and I will make it known,
  that the love with which you loved me
  may be in them and I in them."

The Gospel of the Lord.

Background of the Reading

This passage from the Gospel according to John has been called Jesus' "Priestly Prayer." Jesus calls us, those to whom Jesus made known God's name, a gift to him. He shares the love that the Father has for him with us so that we might share in Jesus' glory. This prayer of loving promise gives comfort to mourners and hope to those who have died. Having offered his love to us, we are to live that love so that others come to know Jesus, know the God who sent him, and share life with him forever.

You might select this reading when the family of the loved one . . .
will be reassured hearing that Christ regards each follower as a gift that will stay with him • will be consoled by the knowledge that God loved each person before the foundation of the world • will be comforted by hearing that followers will be in the presence of the glory of God.

If you select this reading, you might also consider . . .
Lamentations 3:17–26 **(FR–6)** • Acts 10:34–43 or 10:34–36, 42–43 **(FRE–1)** • Psalm 116:5, 6, 10–11, 15–16ac **(RP–7)** • 1 John 3:1–2 **(SR–14)**

G–19

And bowing his head he handed over his spirit.

A reading from the holy Gospel according to John
19:17–18, 25–39

So they took Jesus, and, carrying the cross himself,
  he went out to what is called the Place of the Skull,
  in Hebrew, Golgotha.
There they crucified him, and with him two others,
  one on either side, with Jesus in the middle.

Standing by the cross of Jesus were his mother
  and his mother's sister, Mary the wife of Clopas,
  and Mary Magdalene.
When Jesus saw his mother and the disciple whom he loved,
  he said to his mother, "Woman, behold, your son."
Then he said to the disciple,
  "Behold, your mother."
And from that hour the disciple took her into his home.

After this, aware that everything was now finished,
  in order that the Scripture might be fulfilled,
  Jesus said, "I thirst."
There was a vessel filled with common wine.
So they put a sponge soaked in wine on a sprig of hyssop and put it
    up to his mouth.
When Jesus had taken the wine, he said,
  "It is finished."
And bowing his head, he handed over the Spirit.

Now since it was preparation day,
  in order that the bodies might not remain on the cross on the sabbath,
  for the sabbath day of that week was a solemn one,
  the Jews asked Pilate that their legs be broken
  and they be taken down.
So the soldiers came and broke the legs of the first
  and then of the other one who was crucified with Jesus.

But when they came to Jesus and saw that he was already dead,
   they did not break his legs,
    but one soldier thrust his lance into his side,
    and immediately Blood and water flowed out.
An eyewitness has testified, and his testimony is true;
   he knows that he is speaking the truth,
    so that you also may come to believe.
For this happened so that the Scripture passage might be fulfilled:
   Not a bone of it will be broken.
And again another passage says:
   They will look upon him whom they have pierced.

After this, Joseph of Arimathea,
   secretly a disciple of Jesus for fear of the Jews,
    asked Pilate if he could remove the Body of Jesus.
And Pilate permitted it.
So he came and took his Body.
Nicodemus, the one who had first come to him at night,
   also came bringing a mixture of myrrh and aloes
    weighing about one hundred pounds.

The Gospel of the Lord.

Background of the Reading

John's description of Jesus has complete control. He hands his mother into the beloved disciple's care and vise versa. Mary, as the new Eve, is the mother of all the living. Jesus determines when "it is finished." He hands over his spirit. Blood and water from his side signify Baptism and Eucharist, giving birth to the community that continues his mission. His disciples go right to work: Joseph buries Jesus and Nicodemus honors his body. We do likewise, gathered in Eucharist we pray for our dead.

You might select this reading because your loved one . . .
suffered for a long while before dying • was a mother who had watched a child suffer • witnessed to the faith through difficult times.

If you select this reading, you might also consider . . .
2 Maccabees 12:43–46 (**FR-1**) • Revelation 20:11—21:1 (**FRE-3**) • Psalm 103:8 and 10, 13–14, 15–16, 17–18 (**RP-6**) • Romans 14:7–9, 10c–12 (**SR-6**)

Funeral for
a Baptized Child

The Liturgy of the Word for the Catholic funeral of a baptized child follows the same order as the funerals for adults. You will need to choose the following:

+ First Reading from the Old Testament outside Easter Time (**page 82; BC/FR–1 to BC/FR–2**) or First Reading from the New Testament during Easter Time (**page 84; BC/FRE–1 to BC/FRE–2**)

+ Responsorial Psalm (**page 87; BC/RP–1 to BC/RP–4**)

+ Second Reading (**page 91; BC/SR–1 to BC/SR–5**)

+ Alleluia Verse and Verse before the Gospel (Gospel Acclamation) (**page 96; BC/GA–1 to BC/GA–3**)

+ Gospel (**page 97; BC/G–1 to BC/G–6**)

The readings for the Catholic funeral of a baptized child speak of hope and comfort in our belief that your baptized child shares Christ's victory over death. Think about your child. As you choose readings, you will find that the Scriptures affirm that your child has a share in eternal life and that God is with you in your pain. As your life seems upside down in the days to come, may you find and experience God's grace as he accompanies you.

If you are not sure what reading to choose, your pastor or whomever you are meeting with to prepare the funeral can help.

. . . .

BC/FR-1

He will destroy death for ever.

◊ **A reading from the Book of the Prophet Isaiah**   *25:6a, 7–9*

On this mountain the Lᴏʀᴅ of hosts
    will provide for all peoples.
On this mountain he will destroy
    the veil that veils all peoples,
The web that is woven over all nations;
    he will destroy death forever.
The Lord Gᴏᴅ will wipe away
    the tears from all faces;
The reproach of his people he will remove
    from the whole earth; for the Lᴏʀᴅ has spoken.

    On that day it will be said:
"Behold our God, to whom we looked to save us!
    This is the Lᴏʀᴅ for whom we looked;
    let us rejoice and be glad that he has saved us!"

The Word of the Lord.

Background of the Reading

This reading comes from the first section of the Book of the Prophet Isaiah. It is a hymn of thanksgiving for God's saving love. Isaiah paints a beautiful picture of hope that your child will share fully in God's saving love at the heavenly banquet. God promises to remove anything that separates us from one another and from God. Thus, we can be reunited with your child and all who have gone before us, rejoicing in God's provident and healing love forever.

You might select this reading when the family of the loved one . . .
will be comforted hearing that the Lord came to save us once for all time •
will be reassured with the knowledge that the Lord will provide for his people •
will be consoled hearing that their child is where death does not have a place.

If you select this reading, you might also consider . . .
Psalm 23:1–3, 4, 5, 6 (**BC/RP–1**) • Romans 14:7–9 (**BC/SR–2**) • Mark 10:13–16 (**BC/G–2**)

• • • • • • • • •

BC/FR-2

It is good to hope in silence for the saving help of the Lord.

A reading from the Book of Lamentations   *3:22-26*

The favors of the LORD are not exhausted,
  his mercies are not spent;
They are renewed each morning,
  so great is his faithfulness.
My portion is the LORD, says my soul;
  therefore will I hope in him.

Good is the LORD to one who waits for him,
  to the soul that seeks him;
It is good to hope in silence
  for the saving help of the LORD.

The Word of the Lord.

Background of the Reading

The Book of Lamentations recounts the sufferings of God's people. In the midst of the suffering and great pain one experiences at the death of a child, we need these words of hope. God is always with us—even now. These words invite you to seek the Lord each day. When words do not suffice, hope in silence. The reading reminds us that God's saving help is near to you and your child, who experiences God's merciful and saving love.

You might select this reading when the family of the loved one • • •
will be reassured knowing that God's mercy is never exhausted • needs to hear of the hope that God offers • will be comforted knowing that God is with them in their grief.

If you select this reading, you might also consider • • •
Psalm 42:2, 3, 5cdef; 43:3, 4, 5 **(BC/RP-3)** • Romans 6:3-4, 8-9 **(BC/SR-1)** • Matthew 11:25-30 **(BC/G-1)**

BC/FRE-1

God will wipe away every tear from their eyes.

A reading from the Book of Revelation   *7:9–10, 15–17*

I, John, had a vision of a great multitude,
  which no one could count,
  from every nation, race, people, and tongue.
They stood before the throne and before the Lamb,
  wearing white robes and holding palm branches in their hands.
They cried out in a loud voice:
    "Salvation comes from our God, who is seated on the throne,
      and from the Lamb.

    "For this reason they stand before God's throne
      and worship him day and night in his temple.
    The One who sits on the throne will shelter them.
    They will not hunger or thirst anymore,
      nor will the sun or any heat strike them.
    For the Lamb who is in the center of the throne
      will shepherd them
      and lead them to springs of life-giving water,
      and God will wipe away every tear from their eyes."

The Word of the Lord.

Background of the Reading

The author of the Book of Revelation paints the picture of a joyful, heavenly liturgy. Many people, too many to count, are gathered before the throne of the Lamb of God, singing a hymn of praise and thanksgiving for God's saving love. Jesus, the Lamb, now shepherds, shelters, and feeds them. The life-giving water recalls Baptism and the freedom from pain and suffering it promises. Your child is part of this scene. We believe that one day we will be too.

You might select this reading when the family of the loved one • • •
will be consoled with the knowledge that their child will never be hungry or thirsty, that all of their needs will be met • draws comfort from hearing that God will shepherd their child • will be reassured that the springs of life-giving water provide eternal life.

If you select this reading, you might also consider • • •
Psalm 148:1–2, 11–13a, 13c–14 **(BC/RP–4)** • Romans 6:3–4, 8–9 **(BC/SR–1)** • John 6:51–58 **(BC/G–4)**

• • • • • • • • • • •

BC/FRE-2

There shall be no more death.

A reading from the Book of Revelation   *21:1a, 3-5a*

I, John, saw a new heaven and a new earth.
I heard aloud voice from the throne saying,
  "Behold, God's dwelling is with the human race.
He will dwell with them and they will be his people
  and God himself will always be with them as their God.
He will wipe away every tear from their eyes,
    and there shall be no more death or mourning, wailing or pain,
    for the old order has passed away."

The One who sat on the throne said,
  "Behold, I make all things new."

The Word of the Lord.

Background of the Reading

The author of Revelation gives us a powerful description of the end times. God will dwell with the human race and walk with us like God did at the dawn of Creation. Like the Garden of Paradise, there will be no more fear, tears, death, or mourning. God will make all things new. We wish that we did not have to experience the pain that is now ours. These words offer hope that it will end. They invite those who gather in tears to find comfort in this scene of promise.

You might select this reading when the family of the loved one • • •
will be comforted knowing that God dwells with us in eternal life •
will be consoled hearing that there is a place with no mourning or pain •
needs the assurance of eternal life.

If you select this reading, you might also consider • • •
Psalm 25:4–5ab, 6 and 7bc, 20–21 **(BC/RP-2)** • 1 Corinthians 15:20–23 **(BC/SR–3)** • John 6:37–40 or 6:37–39 **(BC/G–3)**

BC/RP-1 *Psalm 23:1–3, 4, 5, 6 (1)*

R. The Lord is my shepherd; there is nothing I shall want.

The LORD is my shepherd;
  I shall not want.
In verdant pastures
  he gives me repose;
Beside restful waters he leads me;
  he refreshes my soul.
He guides me in right paths
  for his name's sake. **R.**

Even though I walk
  in the dark valley
I fear no evil;
  for you are at my side
With your rod and your staff
  that give me courage. **R.**

You spread the table before me
  in the sight of my foes;
You anoint my head with oil;
  my cup overflows. **R.**

Only goodness and kindness
  follow me
all the days of my life;
And I shall dwell in the house
  of the LORD
for years to come. **R.**

Background of the Reading

Most people know this psalm of confident trust in God as shepherd, a frequent Old Testament image. It offers trust, rest, and refreshment to your little lamb. Verses 5–6 reflect God's offer of food, protection, kindness, and an eternal home to your child. Verse 4 reflects the pain and darkness you might feel and the courage that you need to make it through each day. Psalm 23 is an act of faith in God's promise to shepherd all anointed with God's Spirit, now and always.

You might select this reading when the family of the loved one ● ● ●
finds comfort in the image of God as a shepherd ● will be assured by the images of God leading them to restful waters ● will be consoled by hearing that God will care for their needs.

If you select this reading, you might also consider ● ● ●
Isaiah 25:6a, 7–9 **(BC/FR–1)** ● Revelation 21:1a, 3–5a **(BC/FRE–2)** ● Romans 14:7–9 **(BC/SR–2)** ● John 6:51–58 **(BC/G–4)**

• •

BC/RP-2 *Psalm 25:4–5ab, 6 and 7bc, 20–21 (1)*

R. To you, O Lord, I lift up my soul.

Your ways, O Lᴏʀᴅ, make known to me;
 teach me your paths,
Guide me in your truth and teach me,
 for you are God my savior. **R.**

Remember that your compassion, O Lᴏʀᴅ,
 and your kindness are from of old.
In your kindness remember me,
 because of your goodness, O Lᴏʀᴅ. **R.**

Preserve my life, and rescue me;
 let me not be put to shame, for I take refuge in you.
Let integrity and uprightness preserve me,
 because I wait for you, O Lᴏʀᴅ. **R.**

Background of the Reading

In Psalm 25, a lament psalm, all but one verse starts with a different letter of the Hebrew alphabet. This structure proclaims that all life, from beginning to end, child and adult, leads to God. Verses 4–5 seek God's guidance. Verses 6–7 seek God's compassion. Verses 20–21 ask God to rescue us at this painful time and to persevere in faith, which a child's death can test. Lift up your soul to God. Allow God to fill you—however you need that presence these days.

You might select this reading when the family of the loved one . . .
needs to be assured that God will guide them through their sorrow • will be comforted knowing that God is their refuge during their great sorrow • will be consoled hearing of God's mercy and compassion.

If you select this reading, you might also consider . . .
Lamentations 3:22–26 **(BC/FR–2)** • Revelation 7:9–10, 15–17 **(BC/FRE–1)** • Ephesians 1:3–5 **(BC/SR–4)** • Matthew 11:25–30 **(BC/G–1)**

BC/RP-3   *Psalm 42:2, 3, 5cdef; 43:3, 4, 5 (42:3)*

R. My soul is thirsting for the living God:
  when shall I see him face to face.

As the hind longs for the
    running waters,
so my soul longs for you,
    O God. **R.**

Athirst is my soul for God,
    the living God.
When shall I go and behold
    the face of God? **R.**

I went with the throng
  and led them in procession
    to the house of God.
Amid loud cries of joy
    and thanksgiving,
  with the multitude
    keeping festival. **R.**

Send forth your light and
    your fidelity;
  they shall lead me on
And bring me to your
    holy mountain,
  to your dwelling-place. **R.**

Then will I go in to the altar of God,
    the God of my gladness and joy;
Then will I give you thanks
    upon the harp,
  O God, my God! **R.**

Why are you so downcast,
    O my soul?
  Why do you sigh within me?
Hope in God! For I shall again
    be thanking him,
  in the presence of my savior
    and my God. **R.**

Background of the Reading

The death of a child often increases the human longing for God. Like the psalmist, we want to find the face of God, who can seem absent in the midst of our pain. The final verses of this psalm encourage hope! God promises that sorrow will end and reunion with your child on God's holy mountain will occur. Let the refrain express your pain and your trust in that union with your child and with God.

You might select this reading when the family of the loved one • • •
will draw strength from hearing that our hope is in God • will be comforted to hear that with God there is joy and thanksgiving • will be consoled that God is faithful to his people.

If you select this reading, you might also consider • • •
Lamentations 3:22–26 (BC/FR–2) • Revelation 21:1a, 3–5a (BC/FRE–2) • 1 Thessalonians 4:13–14, 18 (BC/SR–5) • John 6:37–40 or 6:37–39 (BC/G–3)

BC/RP-4 *148:1–2, 11–13a, 13c–14 (13a)*

R. Let all praise the name of the Lord.
Or:
Alleluia.

Praise the LORD from the heavens,
  praise him in the heights;
Praise him, all you his angels,
  praise him, all you his hosts. **R.**

Let the kings of the earth and all peoples,
  the princes and all the judges of the earth,
Young men too, and maidens,
  old men and boys.
Praise the name of the LORD,
  for his name alone is exalted. **R.**

His majesty is above earth and heaven,
  and he has lifted up the horn of his people.
Be this his praise from all his faithful ones,
  from the children of Israel, the people close to him. Alleluia. **R.**

Background of the Reading

Psalm 148 is a hymn of praise to God: The heavens, angels, and all creation, from those in authority and the youngest children, will praise. Just as God has given many gifts to us, so will God lift us up, especially God's chosen ones, who are close to God. This psalm reflects the faith of your child who belonged to God in Baptism and now praises God in the heavens. We praise God for the gift of your child and pray to join him or her, giving praise with the heavenly hosts.

You might select this reading when the family of the loved one . . .
possesses such faith that they draw strength from praising God even in their sorrow • will draw comfort from the praise that all on earth and heaven give God • needs to be reassured that all focus is on the Kingdom of God.

If you select this reading, you might also consider . . .
Isaiah 25:6a, 7–9 (**BC/FR–1**) • Revelation 21:1a, 3–5a (**BC/FRE–2**) • 1 Corinthians 15:20–23 (**BC/SR–3**) • John 19:25–30 (**BC/G–6**)

BC/SR-1

We believe that we shall also live with him.

A Reading from the Letter of Saint Paul to the Romans

6:3–4, 8–9

Brothers and sisters:
Are you unaware that we who were baptized into Christ Jesus
  were baptized into his death?
We were indeed buried with him through baptism into death,
  so that, just as Christ was raised from the dead
  by the glory of the Father,
  we too might live in newness of life.

If, then, we have died with Christ,
  we believe that we shall also live with him.
We know that Christ, raised from the dead, dies no more;
  death no longer has power over him.

The Word of the Lord.

Background of the Reading

Romans 6 reiterates the fact that Baptism unites us intimately with Jesus Christ. Having died with him to sin and the power of evil, including death, we will be raised up as surely as he was. Death has no more power over us. Your baptized child shares in this promise. That gives us reason to trust that he or she shares a new and eternal life with Christ. And one day, so can we.

You might select this reading when the family of the loved one • • •
will be comforted that all who were baptized have gained new life in Christ • will be consoled hearing that death has no power over their child • will draw strength from the assurance that those who have died live with Christ.

If you select this reading, you might also consider • • •
Lamentations 3:22–26 **(BC/FR–2)** • Revelation 7:9–10, 15–17 **(BC/FRE–1)** • Psalm 148:1–2, 11–13a, 13c–14 **(BC/RP–4)** • John 6:51–58 **(BC/G–4)**

• • • • • • • • •

BC/SR-2

Whether we live or die, we are the Lord's.

A reading from the Letter of Saint Paul to the Romans   *14:7–9*

Brothers and sisters:
No one lives for oneself,
  and no one dies for oneself.
For if we live, we live for the Lord,
  and if we die, we die for the Lord;
    so then, whether we live or die, we are the Lord's.
For this is why Christ died and came to life,
  that he might be Lord of both the dead and the living.

The Word of the Lord.

Background of the Reading

Anyone who belongs to Christ is transformed to live for God, not for themselves. This is certainly true for a baptized child. Whether the life of a baptized person is short or long, one lives and dies for the Lord. This reading affirms that truth. Having sought to obey and praise God, your child belongs to Jesus Christ. These words can provide comfort and motivate us to live for the Lord and not simply for ourselves.

You might select this reading when the family of the loved one • • •
needs the assurance that we are the Lord's when we die as well as when we live • will be comforted hearing that Christ's dying and rising made them one with the Lord • will draw strength from hearing that each of us lives for God.

If you select this reading, you might also consider • • •
Isaiah 25:6a, 7–9 **(BC/FR–1)** • Revelation 21:1a, 3–5a **(BC/FRE–2)** •
Psalm 23:1–3, 4, 5, 6 **(BC/RP–1)** • John 19:25–30 **(BC/G–6)**

BC/SR-3

So too in Christ shall all be brought to life.

A reading from the first Letter of Saint Paul to the Corinthians

15:20–23

Brothers and sisters:
Christ has been raised from the dead,
  the firstfruits of those who have fallen asleep.
For since death came through a man,
  the resurrection of the dead came also through man.
For just as in Adam all die,
  so too in Christ shall all be brought to life,
  but each one in proper order:
  Christ the firstfruits;
  then, at his coming, those who belong to Christ.

The Word of the Lord.

Background of the Reading

A favorite theme in St. Paul's writing is to compare Adam and Christ. Death entered the world through Adam. The possibility of eternal life is restored through Christ. Because your child belongs to Christ through Baptism, he or she will be brought to life after Christ, the first to be raised up. And at his coming, all who belong to Christ will join those already sharing his new life. Trust this promise for your child and all who gather to find comfort in these funeral rites.

You might select this reading when the family of the loved one • • •
will be comforted hearing that all will rise from the dead • needs the reassurance that all have life through Christ • will be consoled hearing that because of Christ, we have eternal life.

If you select this reading, you might also consider • • •
Isaiah 25:6a, 7–9 **(BC/FR–1)** • Revelation 21:1a, 3–5a **(BC/FRE–2)** • Psalm 42:2, 3, 5cdef; 43:3, 4, 5 **(BC/RP–3)** • John 11:32–38, 40 **(BC/G–5)**

. . . .

BC/SR-4

He chose us in him, before the foundation of the world, to be holy.

A reading from the Letter of Saint Paul to the Ephesians *1:3–5*

Blessed be the God and Father of our Lord Jesus Christ,
   who has blessed us in Christ
   with every spiritual blessing in the heavens,
   as he chose us in him, before the foundation of the world,
   to be holy and without blemish before him.
In love he destined us for adoption to himself through Jesus Christ,
   in accord with the favor of his will.

The Word of the Lord.

Background of the Reading

This canticle is a song of praise and thanksgiving for the gift of Jesus Christ. Through Baptism into Christ we become God's adopted children. God has chosen us and wills that we be holy—that is, grounded in faith and not in sin. Christ's death and Resurrection have freed us from the power of sin and death. Praise God for sharing that gift with your child and live in ways that show your gratitude for sharing that gift with you, too.

You might select this reading when the family of the loved one . . .
needs the assurance that through Baptism, their child became an adopted child of God • will be comforted hearing that God chose each of us • will be consoled hearing that God loved their child before the foundation of the world.

If you select this reading, you might also consider . . .
Lamentations 3:22–26 **(BC/FR–2)** • Revelation 7:9–10, 15–17 **(BC/FRE–1)** • Psalm 25:4–5ab, 6 and 7bc, 20–21 **(BC/RP–2)** • Mark 10:13–16 **(BC/G–2)**

. . . .

BC/SR-5

We shall be with the Lord forever.

A reading from the first letter of Saint Paul to the Thessalonians
4:13–14, 18

We do not want you to be unaware, brothers and sisters,
  about those who have fallen asleep,
  so that you may not grieve like the rest, who have no hope.
For if we believe that Jesus died and rose,
  so too will God, through Jesus,
  bring with him those who have fallen asleep.
Therefore, console one another with these words.

The Word of the Lord.

Background of the Reading

When this letter was written, people expected Christ's return before anyone living at the time died. But people did die. Paul writes to rekindle hope in the promise of Christ's Resurrection. He also admonishes us to grieve like people with faith in the promise of Resurrection. Death brings pain, so grieve, but grieve with hope. Physical death is not the end. Beyond physical death we will rise with Christ and be with our loved ones forever.

You might select this reading when the family of the loved one . . .
needs the assurance of hope in Christ • will be comforted hearing that God will bring those who have died to him • will be consoled that God continues to look out for those who have died.

If you select this reading, you might also consider . . .
Lamentations 3:22–26 **(BC/FR–2)** • Revelation 21:1a, 3–5a **(BC/FRE–2)** • Psalm 42:2, 3, 5cdef; 43:3, 4, 5 **(BC/RP–3)** • Matthew 11:25–30 **(BC/G–1)**

The Alleluia Verse and Verse before the Gospel (Gospel Acclamation)

• •

You may select one of the following three verses for the Gospel Acclamation. Consult with your music director for musical settings.

BC/GA-1

Blessed are you, Father, Lord of heaven and earth;
you have revealed to the childlike the mysteries of the Kingdom.
—See Matthew 11:25

BC/GA-2

This is the will of my Father, says the Lord,
that I should lose nothing of all that he has given to me,
and that I should raise it up on the last day.
—John 6:39

BC/GA-3

Blessed be the Father of compassion and
God of all encouragement,
who encourages us in our every affliction.
—2 Corinthians 1:3b–41a

BC/G-1

You have hidden these things from the wise and the learned and have revealed them to the childlike.

A reading from the holy Gospel according to Matthew   11:25–30

At that time Jesus answered:
"I give praise to you, Father, Lord
    of heaven and earth,
    for although you have hidden
        these things
    from the wise and the learned
    you have revealed them to
        the childlike.
Yes, Father, such has been your
    gracious will.
All things have been handed over
    to me by my Father.
No one knows the Son except
    the Father,
    and no one knows the Father
        except the Son

and anyone to whom the Son
    wishes to reveal him.

"Come to me, all you who labor
    and are burdened,
and I will give you rest.
Take my yoke upon you and learn
    from me,
    for I am meek and humble
        of heart;
    and you will find rest for
        yourselves.
For my yoke is easy, and my
    burden light."

The Gospel of the Lord.

Background of the Reading

Jesus prays aloud to the Father. He shares a unique and intimate relationship with God, like many children share with a parent. These words tell Jesus' Jewish hearers that God's ways are less burdensome than the Law can feel at times. Even the childlike can know and live God's love. Jesus invites you who carry the burden of your child's death to find rest in him. These words can be reassuring at a time when this burden feels oh so heavy. Turn to him for hope and guidance.

You might select this reading when the family of the loved one • • •
will draw comfort from hearing that God seeks the weary • will be consoled that God has given the childlike the ability to see his ways • needs to hear that they can rest in God.

If you select this reading, you might also consider • • •
Lamentations 3:22–26 **(BC/FR–2)** • Revelation 7:9–10, 15–17 **(BC/FRE–1)** • Psalm 25:4–5ab, 6 and 7bc, 20–21 **(BC/RP–2)** • 1 Thessalonians 4:13–14, 18 **(BC/SR–5)**

The Gospel

• • • • • • • •

BC/G-2
The kingdom of heaven belongs to little children.

A reading from the holy Gospel according to Mark   *10:13–16*

People were bringing children to Jesus that he might touch them,
  but the disciples rebuked them.
When Jesus saw this he became indignant, and said to them,
  "Let the children come to me; do not prevent them,
  for the Kingdom of God belongs to such as these.
Amen, I say to you,
  whoever does not accept the Kingdom of God like a child
  will not enter it."
Then he embraced the children and blessed them,
  placing his hands on them.

The Gospel of the Lord.

Background of the Reading

Mark's account of Jesus is human and inclusive. He says: "Let the children come to me," and embraces them and touches them. In Jesus' day this was radical. Children had little or no value, so for Jesus to act this way was significant. Children naturally trust others and are curious. Follow their example. You probably wish you could embrace, bless, and touch your child again. Trust that Jesus welcomes him or her to heaven. Go to him and invite him to touch you in the pain of your grief.

You might select this reading when the family of the loved one • • •
will be consoled by the special regard God has for children • will draw comfort from hearing that the Kingdom of God belongs to the childlike • needs the assurance that God has a special concern for children.

If you select this reading, you might also consider • • •
Isaiah 25:6a, 7–9 **(BC/FR–1)** • Revelation 21:1a, 3–5a **(BC/FRE–2)** • Psalm 23:1–3, 4, 5, 6 **(BC/RP–1)** • Ephesians 1:3–5 **(BC/SR–4)**

The Gospel

• • • • • • • • •

BC/G-3

This is the will of my Father, that I should not lose anything of what he gave me.

A reading from the holy Gospel according to John

Long form: 6:37–40 [Short form: 6:37–39]

[Jesus said to the crowds:
"Everything that the Father gives me will come to me,
  and I will not reject anyone who comes to me,
  because I came down from heaven not to do my own will
  but the will of the one who sent me.
And this is the will of the one who sent me,
  that I should not lose anything of what he gave me,
  but that I should raise it on the last day.]
For this is the will of my Father,
  that everyone who sees the Son and believes in him
  may have eternal life,
  and I shall raise him on the last day."

The Gospel of the Lord.

Background of the Reading

These words are part of the Bread of Life teaching in John's account of the Gospel. They make clear that Jesus came to do God's will. And God's will is that Jesus not lose anything that God gave him and that Jesus will raise it up on the last day. You showed Jesus to your child. Because of that you can trust that he or she shares in God's promise of eternal life. Find consolation in your gift of faith and in these words.

You might select this reading when the family of the loved one • • •
will be comforted knowing that Christ welcomes all who come to him • will be consoled hearing that Christ will hold on to all who come to him • needs to hear that all who see God will have eternal life.

If you select this reading, you might also consider • • •
Isaiah 25:6a, 7–9 (**BC/FR–1**) • Revelation 21:1a, 3–5a (**BC/FRE–2**) • Psalm 42:2, 3, 5cdef; 43:3, 4, 5 (**BC/RP–3**) • 1 Thessalonians 4:13–14, 18 (**BC/SR–5**)

The Gospel

• • • • • • • •

BC/G-4

(For a child who had already received the Eucharist)

Whoever eats this bread will live forever, and I will raise him up on the last day.

A reading from the holy Gospel according to John   *6:51–58*

Jesus said to the Jews:
"I am the living bread that came down from heaven;
   whoever eats this bread will live forever;
   and the bread that I will give is my Flesh
   for the life of the world."

The Jews quarreled among themselves, saying,
   "How can this man give us his Flesh to eat?"
Jesus said to them,
   "Amen, amen, I say to you,
   unless you eat the Flesh of the Son of Man and drink his Blood,
   you do not have life within you.
Whoever eats my Flesh and drinks my Blood
   has eternal life,
   and I will raise him on the last day.
For my Flesh is true food,
   and my Blood is true drink.
Whoever eats my Flesh and drinks my Blood
   remains in me and I in him.
Just as the living Father sent me
   and I have life because of the Father,
   so also the one who feeds on me
   will have life because of me.
This is the bread that came down from heaven.
Unlike your ancestors who ate and still died,
   whoever eats this bread will live forever."

The Gospel of the Lord.

Background of the Reading

These words are part of the Bread of Life teaching in John's account of the Gospel. God became one with humanity in Christ, God-made-flesh. We become one with God and one another by our sharing in the Eucharist. Having been baptized, your child shares the very life of God, which continues beyond physical death. Feed on Christ at the funeral Mass like your child did in life. Become one with Christ and all who share Communion, living and dead. Taste his healing presence in your brokenness.

You might select this reading when the family of the loved one • • •
will be comforted to know that whoever has taken part in the Eucharist will have eternal life • will be consoled hearing that all who have received Communion remain in Christ • needs to be assured that the family's faithfulness has made a difference.

If you select this reading, you might also consider • • •
Isaiah 25:6a, 7–9 **(BC/FR–1)** • Revelation 7:9–10, 15–17 **(BC/FRE–1)** • Psalm 23:1–3, 4, 5, 6 **(BC/RP–1)** • Romans 6:3–4, 8–9 **(BC/SR–1)**

● ● ● ● ● ● ● ●

BC/G-5

If you believe, you will see the glory of God.

A reading from the holy Gospel according to John   *11:32–38, 40*

When Mary [the sister of Lazarus]
  came to where Jesus was and saw him,
  she fell at his feet and said to him,
  "Lord, if you had been here,
  my brother would not have died."
When Jesus saw her weeping and the Jews had come with her weeping,
  he became perturbed and deeply troubled, and said,
  "Where have you laid him?"
They said to him, "Sir, come and see."
And Jesus wept.
So the Jews said, "See how he loved him."
But some of them said,
  "Could not the one who opened the eyes of the blind man
  have done something so that this man would not have died?"

So Jesus, perturbed again, came to the tomb.
It was a cave, and a stone lay across it.
Jesus said to her,
  "Did I not tell you that if you believe
  you will see the glory of God?"

The Gospel of the Lord.

Background of the Reading

In the Gospel according to John, human encounters reveal Jesus' divinity. Jesus weeps, he feels deeply. His friend died. People grieve, like you grieve at the death of your child. People are frustrated. God did not heal Lazarus. You may be frustrated too. Jesus goes to the tomb and invites faith: "If you believe, you will see the glory of God." By facing feelings and praying to God, like Jesus, you can find him with you in your pain and come to know God's glory, even in the face of the death of a child.

You might select this reading when the family of the loved one • • •
needs to be assured that Christ grieves with the mourning • will draw comfort from hearing that eternal life is for those who believe • will be consoled that death is not final.

If you select this reading, you might also consider • • •
Lamentations 3:22–26 (**BC/FR–2**) • Revelation 7:9–10, 15–17 (**BC/FRE–1**) • Psalm 25:4–5ab, 6 and 7bc, 20–21 (**BC/RP–2**) • 1 Corinthians 15:20–23 (**BC/SR–3**)

The Gospel

BC/G-6
Behold your mother.

A reading from the holy Gospel according to John   *19:25–30*

Standing by the cross of Jesus
   were his mother
and his mother's sister, Mary
   the wife of Clopas,
and Mary Magdalene.
When Jesus saw his mother and
   the disciple whom he loved
he said to his mother, "Woman,
   behold, your son."
Then he said to the disciple,
"Behold, your mother."
And from that hour the disciple
   took her into his home.
After this, aware that everything
   was now finished,
in order that the Scripture might
   be fulfilled,
Jesus said, "I thirst."
There was a vessel filled with
   common wine.
So they put a sponge soaked in
   wine on a sprig of hyssop
and put it up to his mouth.
When Jesus had taken the wine,
   he said,
"It is finished."
And bowing his head, he handed
   over the spirit.

The Gospel of the Lord.

Background of the Reading

John's account presents Jesus as being in control of life and death. He hands his mother over to the beloved disciple and vise versa. He announces, "it is finished," and hands over his spirit. Jesus left neither his mother nor the disciple alone. Jesus does not leave you alone. He is with you. You thirst for your child's physical presence. That thirst can be quenched by finding your child with you in new ways. Place yourself in God's arms. God is with you and your child is with God.

You might select this reading when the family of the loved one • • •
will be comforted from hearing that Jesus gave his mother over to be our mother • will be reassured by hearing that Mary grieved also • draws strength from knowing that Mary, Christ, and the saints are with them in their pain.

If you select this reading, you might also consider • • •
Isaiah 25:6a, 7–9 **(BC/FR–1)** • Revelation 21:1a, 3–5a **(BC/FRE–2)** •
Psalm 148:1–2, 11–13a, 13c–14 **(BC/RP–4)** • Romans 14:7–9 **(BC/SR–2)**

ETERNAL REST IN THE LORD

Funeral for a Child Who Died before Baptism

For a Catholic funeral of a child who died before Baptism, you will need to choose a First Reading from the Old Testament (**page 106; BBC/FR–1 to BBC/FR–2**), an Alleluia Verse and Verse before the Gospel (**page 109; BBC/GA–1 to BBC/GA–3**), and a Gospel (**page 110; BBC/G–1 to BBC/G–3**). Only one Responsorial Psalm is given as an option (**page 108; BBC/RP–1**).

The focus of the readings is the faith of the parents, that in this time of great sorrow, they will be assured of the presence of a loving and comforting God.

Lift up your soul to God. As your life seems upside down in the days to come, may you find and experience God's grace as he accompanies you.

If you are not sure what reading to choose, your pastor or whomever you are meeting with to prepare the funeral can help.

. . . .

BBC/FR-1

He will destroy death forever.

A reading from the Book of the Prophet Isaiah   *25:6a, 7–8*

On this mountain the LORD of hosts
  will provide for all peoples.
On this mountain he will destroy
  the veil that veils all peoples,
The web that is woven over all nations;
  he will destroy death forever.
The Lord GOD will wipe away
  the tears from all faces.

The word of the Lord.

Background of the Reading

From the first section of the Book of the Prophet Isaiah, this reading is a hymn of thanksgiving for God's all-inclusive, saving love. Isaiah paints a picture of hope. Your faith opened the door to faith for your child. God will remove anything that separates us from one another and from God, including death. Your child will dwell on God's holy mountain forever. God provides for all peoples. So trust that your child is with God and that someday we will be too.

You might select this reading when the family of the loved one . . .
will be comforted hearing that every tear will be wiped away • will be consoled that God will remove the veil that separates people from one another • will be strengthened by the assurance that God provides.

If you select this reading, you might also consider . . .
Mark 15:33–46 **(BBC/G-2)**

• • • • • • • • • • •

BBC/FR-2

It is good to hope in silence for the saving help of the Lord.

A reading from the Book of Lamentations   *3:22–26*

The favors of the LORD are not exhausted,
  his mercies are not spent;
They are renewed each morning,
  so great is his faithfulness.
My portion is the LORD, says my soul;
  therefore will I hope in him.

Good is the LORD to one who waits for him,
  to the soul that seeks him;
It is good to hope in silence
  for the saving help of the LORD.

The word of the Lord.

Background of the Reading

The Book of Lamentations recounts the sufferings of God's people. In the midst of the suffering and great pain one can experience at the death of a child, we need these words of hope. God is always with us, for God is the creator of all. Your faith helped your child know God and wait for God's love. Continue to seek the Lord each day. When words do not suffice, hope in silence, for God's merciful and saving love is always near.

You might select this reading when the family of the loved one • • •
will draw strength from hearing that God is available to those who seek him • will be consoled hearing that God is ever merciful • needs to be reassured that there is always hope in God.

If you select this reading, you might also consider • • •
Matthew 11:25–30 (**BBC/G–1**)

BBC/RP-1 *Psalm 25:4–5ab, 6 and 7b, 17 and 20 (1)*

R. To you, O Lord, I lift up my soul.

Your way, O Lord, make known to me;
  teach me your paths.
Guide me in your truth and teach me,
  for you are God my savior. **R.**

Remember that your compassion, O Lord,
  and your kindness are from of old.
In your kindness remember me,
  because of your goodness, O Lord. **R.**

Relieve the troubles of my heart;
  bring me out of my distress.
Preserve my life and rescue me;
  let me not be put to shame, for I take refuge in you. **R.**

Background of the Reading

Psalm 25 is a lament psalm. All but one verse starts with a different letter of the Hebrew alphabet, proclaiming that *all* life, from beginning to end, child and adult, leads to God. Verses 4–5 seek God's guidance. Verses 6–7 seek God's compassion. Verses 17 and 20 ask God to relieve the pain we experience at our child's death. So lift up your soul to God. Invite God's goodness to fill you, guide you, and give you comfort that your faith helps your child.

You might select this reading when the family of the loved one ● ● ●
will draw comfort hearing that our refuge is in the Lord ● needs to be reassured that God is compassionate ● will be consoled and will identify with the pleas to be relieved of distress.

If you select this reading, you might also consider ● ● ●
Psalm 25 is the only option the Church provides for funerals for unbaptized children. It may be used with any reading.

The Alleluia Verse and Verse before the Gospel (Gospel Acclamation)

* *

You may select one of the following two verses for the Gospel Acclamation. Consult with your music director for musical settings.

BBC/GA-1

Blessed be the Father of compassion
and God of all encouragement,
who encourages us in our every affliction.
—2 Corinthians 1:2b–4a

BBC/GA-1

Jesus Christ is the firstborn from the dead;
glory and kingship be his forever and ever. Amen.
—Revelation 1:5a, 6b

The Gospel

. . . .

BBC/G-1

You have hidden these things from the wise
and the learned and have revealed them to the childlike.

A reading from the holy Gospel according to Matthew   *11:25–30*

At that time Jesus answered:
"I give praise to you, Father,
Lord of heaven and earth,
for although you have hidden
these things
from the wise and the learned
you have revealed them to
the childlike.
Yes, Father, such has been your
gracious will.
All things have been handed over
to me by my Father.
No one knows the Son except
the Father,

and no one knows the Father
except the Son
and anyone to whom the Son
wishes to reveal him."

"Come to me, all you who labor
and are burdened,
and I will give you rest.
Take my yoke upon you and learn
from me,
for I am meek and humble of heart;
and you will find rest
for yourselves.
For my yoke is easy, and my
burden light."

The Gospel of the Lord.

Background of the Reading

Jesus prays aloud to God. He shares a unique and intimate relationship with God, like many children share with a parent. Jesus showed us that God's ways are less burdensome than leaders taught in his day. The childlike can know and live God's love. Your relationship with Jesus invited your child to come to him. Call on that faith. Go to him in hope and for guidance, as you carry the burden of your child's death. Find rest and reassurance in God when this burden feels so heavy.

You might select this reading when the family of the loved one . . .
will be comforted that God will relieve them of their burdens • will be consoled by the regard that God has for children • needs to be assured that rest can be found in God.

If you select this reading, you might also consider . . .
Lamentations 3:22–26 **(BBC/FR–2)**

. . . .

BBC/G-2

Jesus gave a loud cry and breathed his last.

A reading from the holy Gospel according to Mark   *15:33-46*

At noon darkness came over the whole land
  until three in the afternoon.
And at three o'clock Jesus cried out in a loud voice,
  "Eloi, Eloi, lema sabachthani?"
  which is translated,
  "My God, my God, why have you forsaken me?"
Some of the bystanders who heard it said,
  "Look, he is calling Elijah."
One of them ran, soaked a sponge with wine, put it on a reed,
  and gave it to him to drink, saying,
  "Wait, let us see if Elijah comes to take him down."
Jesus gave a loud cry and breathed his last.
The veil of the sanctuary was torn in two from top to bottom.
When the centurion who stood facing him
  saw how he breathed his last he said,
  "Truly this man was the Son of God!"
There were also women looking on from a distance.
Among them were Mary Magdalene,
  Mary the mother of the younger James, and of Joses, and Salome.
These women had followed him when he was in Galilee
  and ministered to him.
There were also many other women
  who had come up with him to Jerusalem.

When it was already evening,
  since it was the day of preparation,
  the day before the sabbath, Joseph of Arimathea,
  a distinguished member of the council,
  who was himself awaiting the Kingdom of God,
  came and courageously went to Pilate
  and asked for the Body of Jesus.
Pilate was amazed that he was already dead.

He summoned the centurion
    and asked him if Jesus had already died.
And when he learned of it from the centurion,
    he gave the Body to Joseph.
Having bought a linen cloth, he took him down,
    wrapped him in the linen cloth,
      and laid him in a tomb that had been hewn out of the rock.
Then he rolled a stone against the entrance of the tomb.

The Gospel of the Lord.

Background of the Reading

Mark's account of Jesus is very human. He quotes familiar words from Psalm 22—a cry of trust that God affirms his life. He cries out in pain at the point of death. The women stay with and support him. A nonbeliever, the centurion, calls him Son of God and confirms his death for Pilate. Even without Baptism, your child can know Jesus because of the faith you shared with her or him. These words of hope affirm the power of God's unconditional love. Support each other with them.

You might select this reading when the family of the loved one • • •
will be comforted hearing that the Son of God also suffered and died • will draw strength from knowing that Jesus had friends who kept a vigil as he died • will be consoled knowing that Christ's suffering was united to their child's suffering and death.

If you select this reading, you might also consider • • •
Isaiah 25:6a, 7–8 **(BBC/FR–1)**

. . . .

BBC/G-3

Behold your mother.

A reading from the holy Gospel according to John   *19:25–30*

Standing by the cross of Jesus
were his mother
and his mother's sister,
Mary the wife of Clopas,
and Mary Magdalene.
When Jesus saw his mother and
the disciple whom he loved
he said to his mother, "Woman,
behold, your son."
Then he said to the disciple,
"Behold, O mother."
And from that hour the disciple
took her into his home.

After this, aware that everything
was now finished,
in order that the Scripture
might be fulfilled,
Jesus said, "I thirst."
There was a vessel filled with
common wine.
So they put a sponge soaked in
wine on a sprig of hyssop
and put it up to his mouth.
When Jesus had taken the wine,
he said,
"It is finished."
And bowing his head,
he handed over the spirit.

The Gospel of the Lord.

Background of the Reading

John's account presents Jesus having control over life and death. He hands his mother over to the beloved disciple and vise versa. Mary is the new Eve, the mother of *all* the living. She is your mother and mother of your deceased child. Neither of you are alone. Jesus is with you. He announces: "it is finished," handing over his spirit. You thirst for your child's physical presence. Quench your thirst. Find your child with you in new ways. Discover that God is always with you and your child.

You might select this reading when the family of the loved one . . .
will draw comfort from a feeling of solidarity with Mary, who also witnessed her child's death • will be consoled that Jesus gave his mother to all of us • needs to be assured that Jesus died for our sins.

If you select this reading, you might also consider . . .
Lamentations 3:22–26 **(BBC/FR–2)**

The Prayer of the Faithful

At a Catholic funeral, the Prayer of the Faithful (also called the Universal Prayer) takes place after the homily and concludes the Liturgy of the Word. This prayer presents a series of petitions for the needs of the Church, the world, the oppressed or afflicted, and the local community. At a funeral, petitions may be included for the needs of the grieving family and for the repose of the soul of their deceased loved one. This prayer is a good reminder that we do not pray simply for ourselves during sad times—we pause and remember in prayer the world of which we are a part, and for which we have a responsibility as Christian believers. The prayer may be spoken or sung; the response may also be spoken or sung. Your parish priest, deacon, or music and liturgy director will also be able to help you.

This section provides sample texts you may use at the funeral liturgy and guidance for either adapting the sample prayers or composing your own.

The Structure of the Prayer of the Faithful

The Prayer of the Faithful (or Universal Prayer) follows the same structure at every liturgy. The presider of the liturgy introduces the prayer; a deacon or reader pronounces the petitions for the needs of the Church, the world, the oppressed, and the local community to which the assembly responds; and the presider sums up the petitions with a concluding prayer. The following texts may be used at the funeral of your loved one or may serve as a model for composing your own prayers so that they are crafted especially to the needs of your family and parish community.

The parts of the prayer are bold. The directions for writing the prayer are italic. Sample prayers are centered text.

Introduction

Notice that this is not a prayer addressed to God, but an invitation to prayer addressed to all present. It is read by the priest (at Mass) or deacon (outside of Mass) presiding at the funeral liturgy.

Trusting in God's care for those who have died

and for those who mourn,

we lift up our prayers for the Church and the world.

Petitions

The petitions always follow the same pattern: We pray for the Church, the world, the oppressed and the afflicted, and the local community. Additional petitions may be added. The petitions are read or chanted by the deacon, reader (usually a family member or friend), or parish cantor. When writing the petitions, consider how the subject (Church, world, etc.) relates to the general needs of death and eternal life.

For the Church:

For the Church,
that leaders and laity be ever ready
to carry out the Church's work of burying the dead,
consoling those who mourn,
and praying for all who have gone before,
making known Christ's mercy and salvation to all,
we pray to the Lord:

For the World:

For leaders of all nations,
that they might be vigorous in alleviating suffering—
striving to ensure resources for medical research,
for a high standard of health care,
and for compassionate end-of-life care for all people,
we pray to the Lord:

For the Oppressed and the Afflicted:

For those who die alone or among strangers,
those who die homeless, in poverty,
those who die far from home,
or those who die fleeing from violence or
oppressive situations,
may the Holy Spirit give them strength and hope
and rouse us to provide them aid and comfort, we pray to the Lord:

For the Local Community:

For the people of [*name of parish, school, town, or other community*]
that they might rejoice in the gift of **N.**_____'s life,
persevere in faithful service, and look forward
to meeting again in the heavenly Kingdom,
we pray to the Lord:

For care givers, health care workers, and all those they serve,
that they might feel Christ's compassion and healing presence
in each encounter, we pray to the Lord:

Additional Petitions:

For all
[*names of special interests or concerns of the deceased*]
who serve faithfully,
may they be strengthened by God's presence with them each day
and encouraged by the appreciation of those they serve,
we pray to the Lord:

For all who mourn **N.**_____'s passing
that the pain of separation may be calmed
by the hope of reunion in the Resurrection,
we pray to the Lord:

For all who have died, especially **N.**_____,
who trusted in Christ's mercy
and is now wrapped in the great mystery beyond our understanding,
that he/she be welcomed into his/her true home
and find peace and joy in God's presence,
we pray to the Lord:

Response of the Assembly

*The response to each petition by those attending the funeral liturgy is
an important part of the prayer. Although it may be newly composed,
in order that the assembly can better participate, it is best if you use
a response that most will know, such as:* Lord, hear our prayer.

Concluding Prayer

*The presiding priest or deacon will conclude the Prayer of the Faithful
with a short prayer. A simple way to construct this prayer is to use
this format:* **You, Who, Do, Through**. *Address this prayer to God,
the Father (*You*), and note that he acts in a particular way* (**Who**).
Indicate something the Father or Son has done or will do for us (**Do**),
and conclude with the ending found in the example below (**Through**).

YOU: Father of all mercy,

WHO: who longs to welcome us into your presence

DO: make us eager to do your work on earth
and always mindful of our true home in you.

THROUGH: Through Christ our Lord.

Amen.

Assistance from Parish Staff

*There is no need to compose all parts of the Prayer of the Faithful.
You may just wish to compose the petitions. This is perfectly
acceptable, especially during this time of grief. Your parish priest,
deacon, and music and/or liturgy director will certainly understand
that this is an overwhelming time for you and will be able to help
prepare an introduction and concluding prayer for you. After
composing the parts of the Prayer of the Faithful, you will want
to be sure to give the texts to your parish staff to review and give
to whomever will be reading the petitions at the funeral liturgy.*

ETERNAL REST IN THE LORD
Preparing the Liturgy of the Word at Catholic Funerals

NAME OF DECEASED PERSON: _____

DATE OF BIRTH: _____ DATE OF DEATH: _____

NAME OF FAMILY MEMBER(S)
PREPARING FUNERAL: _____

RELATIONSHIP   PHONE
TO THE DECEASED: _____ NUMBER: _____

CHURCH: _____

DATE OF FUNERAL LITURGY: _____ TIME OF FUNERAL LITURGY: _____

PRESIDING MINISTER: _____

Selection Form

After you have selected the Scripture readings you would like to have proclaimed at the funeral liturgy for your loved one, you will need to record them on this form and give it to the priest or deacon who will be presiding at the funeral Mass or liturgy without Mass. Write the number of the readings you have chosen on the lines below (for example, **FR–1**). You may use this page or download an editable PDF from this website: www.LTP.org/s /EERL_form (click on the "Supplement" tab).

THE READINGS
The First Reading from the Old Testament _____

The readings for adults are found on pages 1–9. The readings for baptized children are found on pages 82–83. The readings for unbaptized children are found on pages 106–107.

The First Reading from the
New Testament during Easter Time _____

The readings for adults are found on pages 11–16. The readings for baptized children are found on pages 84–86.

The Responsorial Psalm _____

The psalms for adults are found on pages 17–27. The psalms for baptized children are found on pages 87–90. The psalm for unbaptized children is found on page 108.

The Second Reading _____

The readings for adults are found on pages 29–47. The readings for baptized children are found on pages 91–95. The Second Reading for unbaptized children may be omitted.

The Gospel Acclamation _____

The acclamations for adults are found on pages 49–50. The acclamations for baptized children are found on page 96. The acclamations for unbaptized children are found on page 109.

The Gospel _____

The readings for adults are found on pages 51–80. The readings for baptized children are found on pages 97–104. The readings for unbaptized children are found on pages 110–113.

PRAYER OF THE FAITHFUL

If you will be composing any or all parts of the Prayer of the Faithful, be sure to e-mail the presider and the reader a copy prior to the liturgy. Sample texts are found on pages 116–119.